# Elinor Ostrom

# Elinor Ostrom

## An Intellectual Biography

Vlad Tarko

ROWMAN & LITTLEFIELD
INTERNATIONAL
London • New York

Published by Rowman & Littlefield International Ltd
Unit A, Whitacre Mews, 26-34 Stannary Street, London SE11 4AB
www.rowmaninternational.com

Rowman & Littlefield International Ltd. is an affiliate of Rowman & Littlefield
4501 Forbes Boulevard, Suite 200, Lanham, Maryland 20706, USA
With additional offices in Boulder, New York, Toronto (Canada), and
Plymouth (UK)
www.rowman.com

**British Library Cataloguing in Publication Data**
A catalogue record for this book is available from the British Library

ISBN: HB 978-1-7834-8588-8
      PB 978-1-7834-8589-5

**Library of Congress Cataloging-in-Publication Data is Available**

ISBN 978-1-78348-588-8 (cloth: alk. paper)
ISBN 978-1-78348-589-5 (pbk: alk. paper)
ISBN 978-1-78348-590-1 (electronic)

♾™ The paper used in this publication meets the minimum requirements of
American National Standard for Information Sciences—Permanence of Paper for
Printed Library Materials, ANSI/NISO Z39.48-1992.

Printed in the United States of America

# Contents

# List of Figures

# List of Photos

# List of Tables

# Acknowledgments

My first contact with the ideas of the Bloomington School came about nine years ago when I first volunteered, and then was hired by the Center for Institutional Analysis and Development (CADI), in Bucharest, Romania. My work there alongside Horia Terpe, Ionut Sterpan, Aura Matei, and others was deeply rewarding and also led to meeting Paul Dragos Aligica. My collaboration with him started while I was still at CADI, but soon greatly expanded as he urged me to do a PhD in economics at George Mason University (GMU), and still continues to this day. I've benefitted greatly from Dragos' constant intellectual challenges. At GMU my engagement with these ideas, combined with further interest in the theory of entrepreneurship and broader public choice and institutionalist theories, reached a whole new level. My gratitude goes especially to Peter Boettke whose enthusiasm for economics is highly contagious, and who is always reminding us that economics is not just fun, but also a very serious game with major real-world consequences. His synthesis of Bloomington School ideas with Virginia School Public Choice and Austrian market-process/entrepreneurship theory has greatly influenced my own thinking. Virgil Storr and Chris Coyne have created an amazing intellectual environment at the Mercatus Graduate Student Paper Workshop, where Bloomington School ideas are often discussed. My own thinking and writing about coproduction and polycentricity have greatly benefited from the skeptical push-back from Peter Leeson as part of this workshop, as well as from Richard Wagner's ideas about "entangled political economy,"

which provide an original interpretation of the Ostromian critique
of the "markets versus states" dichotomy. Apart from Mercatus, I've
also greatly benefited from contacts over the last few years with the
Bloomington Workshop, at the WOW5 conference, at the Public Choice
Society conference, and at the Polycentricity Workshop in Bloomington
organized by Andreas Thiel and Bill Blomquist. I've particularly benefitted from discussions with Robert Bish, William Blomquist, Bryan
Bruns, Roberta Herzberg, Anas Malik, Graham Marshall, Filippo
Sabetti, Edella Schlager, and Andreas Thiel.
    Many thanks to all of you!

# Introduction

## The Idea of Self-Governance as the Foundation of Institutional Analysis and Development

They thought it would be more fun to build their own furniture. They didn't know how, of course, but they knew whom to ask. Paul Goodman, a Unionville carpenter, taught them how to cut the wood and assemble it. And he taught them that there is a lot more to carpentry than just cutting and assembling. He showed them how to use the natural patterns in the wood, how to let the wood guide them, and how to embed its idiosyncrasies into their design. Rather than hiding the large circular marks recording the tree's history and growth, they used them to give a unique look to their table. They were particularly happy with this result.

The carpentry lesson and practice gave them an epiphany. This is how social science research should also be done! Hands on and learning from those you study, rather than detached and pretending to be coldly observing. They called their new research center at Indiana University in Bloomington, The Workshop in Political Theory and Policy Analysis. And it, indeed, developed like no other research center. As Elinor Ostrom remembered,

> One of the reasons we called this place a workshop instead of a center was because of working with Paul and understanding what artisanship was. You might be working on something like a cabinet and thinking about the design of it, and thinking this idea versus that idea, and then Paul could pick up a board and say, oh, you shouldn't use this one because it will split. He could see things in wood that we couldn't. So the whole idea of artisans and apprentices and the structure of a good workshop really made an impression on us. (Leonard 2009)

1

Photo 1.   *Elinor Ostrom Showing James Buchanan Her Copy
of* The Calculus of Consent. *(Source: Elinor Ostrom Collection, The Lilly Library)*

This book is about the birth and growth of this center, focusing mainly on the ideas of its creators and leaders, Vincent and Elinor Ostrom, but bearing in mind that their philosophical and scientific efforts have been successful partly because they have managed to inspire and take part in a large network of like-minded scholars, a network that continues to thrive and grow after their departure. They started the Workshop in 1973, after setting up a series of informal weekly meetings since 1969. It became a major international, interdisciplinary research center and a key actor in the rise of New Institutionalism and public choice economics (Mitchell 1988).

Over the years, the Ostroms received offers from Harvard and Duke, but they decided to remain at Indiana: "my sense has been that you don't build something like this [Workshop] and just move it," explained Elinor Ostrom. "Part of the staff are not movable. They understand the enterprise and they make a difference. We've had faculty colleagues who were just great. We have a team and you don't pick up and move a whole team" (Zagorski 2006). When she won the Nobel Prize in Economics in 2009, she donated the money to the workshop, saying that the research honored by the prize had been a collective effort.

Naming their research center a "workshop" also had the added advantage that it avoided all university bureaucratic categories. Universities set up "centers," which have "programs," and they have predefined rules for what a "center" can do, and for what a "program" is. The Ostrom Workshop was able to be set up as an independent entity, housed at the University of Indiana Bloomington, but operating under its own rules. This, too, is something that they've noted and emphasized in their studies—that people often find ways around problems, creating their own rules, when formal institutions don't necessarily help or when they may even hamper their efforts.

One of the challenges looking forward is to preserve the Elinor–Vincent intellectual dynamic, which has been at the core of the development of the workshop. As Elinor Ostrom noted, "[t]here is no way you can write about my work without paying attention to Vincent" (Toonen 2010). Some of the ideas associated with Elinor Ostrom were actually first developed by Vincent. For instance, "it should not be overlooked that it was Vincent, not me [Elinor], who discovered and first used the concept of common-pool resources in his teaching and writing on common property resource management at the end of the 1950s" (Toonen 2010). But their intellectual temperaments have been so different that this poses a significant challenge to the student of their work. To fully grasp the achievements and depth of the Bloomington School, one needs to be willing to enjoy the ride from Vincent Ostrom's philosophical inquiries into the nature and vulnerabilities of self-governance, including his reflections on the importance of language and textual reinterpretation, and all the way to Elinor Ostrom's multipage diagrams trying to capture the details of on-the-ground institutional arrangements and synthesize hundreds of case studies.

## OVERCOMING PREJUDICE

Elinor Claire Awan was born in 1933 and grew up in the midst of the Great Depression in Los Angeles. When her parents divorced, she remained with her mother and lived in relatively poor conditions, having to grow their own food in their backyard garden. She went to Beverly Hills High School, across the street from her house. "I'm very grateful for that opportunity," she later recalled, "because 90 percent of the kids who went to Beverly Hills High School went on to college. I don't think

I would have gone to college if not for being in that environment." She recalled that her "mother didn't want me to go to college—[she] saw no reason whatsoever to do that" (Sullivan 2011). Despite this, she went to University of California, Los Angeles (UCLA) and graduated in 1954 with a major in political science.

In college she also met her first husband, Charles Scott. After graduation, they moved to Boston, where she worked as an assistant personnel manager at a law firm, while Charles went to Harvard's law school. "Basically I put my husband through law school," she recalled (Leonard 2009). They returned to the Los Angeles area and she obtained a job at UCLA at the personnel office. After deciding to take a course in public administration, more or less as a hobby, she became so fascinated with the subject matter that she ended up getting a Master's degree and a PhD in political science. At the time, this was quite unusual for a woman. As she recalled, "I was thinking of going to graduate school and was strongly discouraged because I would never be able to do anything but teach in a city college" (Smith 2009). Her own husband objected to her getting a PhD, which led her to divorce him. "She recalls this without bitterness, adding that she also found the life of a corporate lawyer's wife unappealing. She physically shuddered when she recalled the parties that she had to attend, with all the men in one room and all the wives in another" (Wilson 2016).

"The '50s and '60s were not very good for academic women, or women in business or other fields. But things have changed quite a bit. Thank goodness!" (Sullivan 2011). She hoped that her recognition would open the door for more women: "I've attended economic sessions where I've been the only woman in the room, but that is slowly changing and I think there's a greater respect now that women can make a major contribution. And I would hope that the recognition here is helping that along" (Smith 2009).

Prior to winning the Nobel Prize, she had been a founding member and president of the Public Choice Society (1982–84), president of the American Political Science Association (1996–97), and one of the founding members of the International Association for the Study of the Commons. She was the first woman to receive the Johan Skytte Prize (1999), as well as the William H. Riker Prize (2008) in political science, and won other prestigious awards such as the Frank E. Seidman Distinguished Award for Political Economy (1998), the John J. Carty Award from the National Academy of Sciences (2004), and the James

Madison Award by the American Political Science Association (2005). With the exception to her long-term association with the Public Choice Society, most of her affiliations were to political science, rather than economics. But her work has been multidisciplinary from the very beginning.

Her PhD dissertation was about water management in California, setting her on course on what would become a lifelong study of how communities self-organize in response to various challenges. "On my dissertation committee, I had political scientists, economists, sociologists, a water engineer and a geologist," she recalled. "My work was then, and has always been, interdisciplinary. Some universities don't get students started on thinking in an interdisciplinary way, so that's one of the strengths of UCLA" (Sullivan 2011).

In 1963, she married fellow political scientist Vincent Ostrom, but they did not remain at UCLA due to a conflict that Vincent had with the university (see Chapter 1). The couple moved to Indiana University Bloomington a year later.

## BASIC PRINCIPLES OF
## INSTITUTIONAL ECONOMICS

### What Are Institutions?

This is the first lesson in institutional economics: To understand what happens in a society, you have to understand its rules and norms, but bear in mind that what matters are the de facto rules, which often depart from or go far beyond what is written on some pieces of paper.

For example, in their studies of ecological conservation, Elinor Ostrom and her collaborators sometimes found government planners gathered around a large map in some capital, far away from the place where the problem actually was. These planners would be gravely pointing to various administrative regions on the map, delineated by carefully drawn borders. They would talk about who is responsible for what in each of these regions. It all sounded very professional. But any good scientist is a potential trouble maker, letting their curiosity and their desire to understand things in detail take the lead and guide them to an unpredictable destination. So, when the Ostroms and their colleagues would actually go to check the reality on the ground, they would sometimes discover that the locals had no idea whatsoever about any border supposedly going through their land. Such careful lines on the planners' maps were "rules-in-form," but they were *not* the "rules-in-use." Such empty rules-in-form are obviously quite ridiculous, but that does not mean that some people don't mistakenly take them for the real thing, often with highly unfortunate consequences.

If you think about the world around you, and carefully observe how people act, you will no doubt be able to find many examples of rules-in-form that depart, more or less, from the actual rules-in-use. From the speed limits that almost no one obeys to the unwritten, and yet very real, informal norms that keep the scientific community working. Perhaps sometimes you yourself act like the silly planners above, either confused by what you thought the rules were and embarrassingly discovering that only suckers take seriously some of the "rules," or, on the contrary, finding out the hard way that you've ignored some serious rule-in-use that no one has previously bothered telling you about—but ignorance of the unwritten law is no excuse. Of course, most of the time, it is by making such errors that we gradually learn what the rules-in-use actually are.

To understand the social world, you need to discover the rules-in-use—those rules that are actually monitored and enforced in one way or another. It is these rules-in-use that actually punish or reward certain actions and, hence, guide human behavior in some directions and away from others. It is such rules-in-use, operating upon many people, which explain the aggregate social, economic, and political outcomes that we observe to occur. Good social scientists are like tourists who have yet to familiarize with the local rules or a little bit like children, asking funny questions about what everyone else just takes for granted.

When we refer to "institutions" we refer to complex networks of such rules-in-use. As Elinor Ostrom (2005a, 3) has put it,

> To understand institutions one needs to know what they are, how and why they are crafted and sustained, and what consequences they generate in diverse settings. Understanding anything is a process of learning what it does, how and why it works, how to create or modify it, and eventually how to convey that knowledge to others. Broadly defined, institutions are the prescriptions that humans use to organize all forms of repetitive and structured interactions including those with families, neighborhoods, markets, firms, sports, leagues, churches, private associations, and governments at all scales.

As a result of building upon the basic lesson described above, and exploring its consequences across a wide variety of different empirical cases, the Bloomington School has become one of the most important intellectual centers of "New Institutional Economics" (NIE). Other prominent NIE scholars, whose work has influenced the Bloomington School, have been Ronald Coase (Nobel Prize in 1991), Douglass North (Nobel Prize in 1993), and Oliver Williamson (sharing the Nobel Prize with Elinor Ostrom in 2009). These scholars, and many others who have built upon their work, ended up differentiating themselves from the "Old Institutionalism," put forward by Thorstein Veblen, Wesley Mitchell, or John R. Commons, by the fact that they explained institutions by appealing to how *individuals* behave and interact. The focus is on the fact that "[i]ndividuals interacting within rule-structured situations face choices regarding the actions and strategies they take, leading to consequences for themselves and for others" (Elinor Ostrom 2005a, 3). This is known as "methodological individualism"—we are interested in understanding social phenomena, but we are going to understand them by ultimately looking at how *individuals'* behavior is affected by the formal and informal rules.

## Transaction Costs

Coase and Williamson built a perspective on institutions known as "transaction cost economics." Transaction costs refer to the fact that all cooperative interactions between people, from simple trading on a market to complex collective agreements, take time and effort. The second lesson of institutional economics is that *all institutions, be they formal rules or informal norms, are created and persist because they are useful mechanisms for economizing upon transaction costs.*

To see why this is so, imagine the contrary. Imagine we could always achieve agreement instantaneously and without effort, and that no uncertainty about the future would exist. Such a world would be completely different from our world. Instead of bargaining by trial and error until we find a mutually acceptable deal, we would instantaneously hit upon the optimal deal, perhaps by reading each other minds. Instead of bitterly fighting until we discover what the true balance of power is, we would just jump to the conclusion without wasting time and resources in actual fighting. Instead of engaging in contracts and long-term agreements, that is, agreeing to behavioral constraints benefiting us only on

average, despite occasional cases when we would get the short end
of the deal, we would only make on-the-spot deals and, if conditions
would change, we would immediately be able to find new partners and
agree upon new deals. No organizations, firms, or marriages would
exist either, but only separate individuals constantly rearranging their
patterns of interactions, continuously choosing the perfectly efficient
outcome.[1] No social norms and communities would exist either because
we would know how to interact with each person individually, so there
would be no need for highly aggregated heuristics that only work on
average. If we know exactly what each person wants, and what they're
capable of doing, we don't need the aggregated information about what
"people in general" tend to like and about how they are most likely to
respond to various acts. No laws would exist either because everyone
would constantly get the best outcome that they could possibly get, by
force or bargaining, and they would know it. There would be no need
for general rules, as all activities would be completely individualized. In
brief, without transaction costs there would be *no* institutions.

A hypothetical world of zero transaction costs is, thus, a world
without conflicts, without contracts and bargaining, without organizations, without social norms, and without laws. A zero transaction costs
world, no matter how complex, would be in a perpetual "Nash equilibrium," that is, a world where no one ever has second thoughts about
their choices. This, though experimental, is of course useful precisely
because we live in a world where often very large transaction costs
exist. By thinking about what would happen if transaction costs were
zero, we can understand why various institutions are created in the real
world and what functions they play. These institutions are imperfect and
incomplete shortcuts toward the zero-transaction costs world in which
no resources are ever wasted. For instance, institutions such as private
property help in preventing a wide range of conflicts from appearing
in the first place, and effective conflict resolution mechanisms, such as
good courts, help people waste the least amount of time and money in
actual fighting.

The fact that transaction costs exist also means that it is usually difficult, or even impossible, to discover the best institutions; that is, the best
available shortcuts toward the most efficient world, which satisfies everyone's wishes as well as possible. If you think of the zero-transaction
costs world as the set of all possible goods and services that we could in
principle have, given our level of technology and our natural resources,

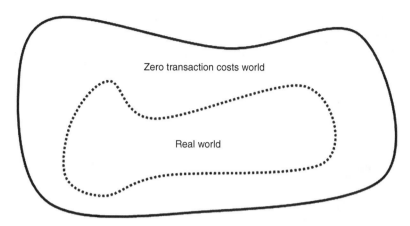

**Figure I.1. Transaction Cost Economics Perspective on Efficiency.**

the real world is a smaller subset in it because not all beneficial deals can be discovered and secured (Figure I.1). Institutions set the frontier of how much the real world can expand toward the hypothetical perfect efficiency of the zero-transaction costs world. As Mancur Olson (1996) put it, billions of dollars are left on the sidewalk, and exactly how many of those bills escape us depends on the quality of our institutions.

One particular theory of the transaction costs involved in collective action played a crucial role in the intellectual origins of the Bloomington School. In 1962, public choice, and what became known as constitutional political economy, entered the world of economics and political science with a splash as James Buchanan and Gordon Tullock published *The Calculus of Consent*. James Buchanan received a Nobel Prize in 1986 for his contributions to public choice, and he was a long-time inspiration and friend to the Ostroms.

As Vincent and Elinor Ostrom remember, their research program got off the ground thanks to *The Calculus of Consent*, which "gave us basic tools for acquiring some analytical leverage in addressing particular problems that people are required to address about public affairs" (Elinor Ostrom and Ostrom 2004). In particular, the "principle of conceptual unanimity gave meaning to what [we] had observed and what was accomplished" (Elinor Ostrom and Ostrom 2004). By "conceptual unanimity," Buchanan and Tullock meant that (a) in a zero-transaction costs world in which we assume away violence, all collective decisions could be taken by unanimity, such that, thanks to Coasian bargainings and compensations for the nay-sayers, setting the stage for the unanimous decision, no one would be harmed; and (b) the departures from unanimity, which cause uncompensated harms to some part of the population, are justified only by the prohibitive transaction costs of organizing and enforcing collective decision making. In other words, if it is relatively easy to consult with the people affected by an issue, a closer to full consensus approach should be favored. Conversely, if jurisdictions only cause small externalities upon one another, it is inefficient to centralize decision making—hence increasing the transaction costs of collective action.

The Ostroms interpreted their empirical findings through this theoretical lens. For instance, when studying water management in West Basin, California, for her PhD, Elinor Ostrom found that adjudicating water rights was driven by intuitive considerations of "equity jurisprudence," which can be understood as seeking "to achieve conceptual unanimity in establishing the nature of the problem, in adjudicating water rights, in formulating the rules that were constitutive of water user associations, the way they related to one another, and in monitoring performance" (Elinor Ostrom and Ostrom 2004).

The calculus of consent logic puts a limit on collective decision making, sometimes requiring greater levels of consensus than simple majority rule, as well as a limit on centralization. Vincent Ostrom's *The Political Theory of the Compound Republic* (V. Ostrom 1987) is built on this calculus of consent account of federalism. And as Elinor Ostrom (2011b) recalled:

> A fundamental lesson that we all learned from Buchanan and Tullock is captured on page 114 of *Calculus of Consent* where they state: "both decentralization and size factors suggest that when possible, collective action should be organized in small rather than large political units. Organizations in large units may be justified only by the overwhelming importance of the externalities that remain after localized and decentralized collectivization." I wish I could get that quote put on a poster to be hung on a wall of every university I visit as well as integrated into the textbooks on public policy and urban governance! Somehow, many social scientists have forgotten this core idea.

As we'll see in the following chapters, this "core idea" has indeed been at the forefront of all of the debates in which the Bloomington School has engaged.

The calculus of consent is also important for providing a particular theory of how communities form, based on the idea that individuals accept membership to a community because the benefits they receive outweigh the personal costs of having to obey some collective decisions with which they disagree (see also Buchanan 1987). Such a theory may appear at first glance to be too simple and overly economic, but we can use it in a more sophisticated fashion as a tool for analyzing the legitimacy of rules, how this legitimacy may get eroded, and the factors that may undermine people's sense of belonging. This has been a key concern for Vincent Ostrom (1997) when he analyzed the "vulnerabilities of democracies," and is a key concern for "civic studies" (Elkin and Soltan 2007; Levine and Soltan 2014). In any case, regardless of whether one accepts this particular account of community membership, having such a theory is essential:

> Until a theoretical explanation—based on human choice—for self-organized and self-governed enterprises is fully developed and accepted...one cannot predict or explain when individuals will be able to solve a common problem through self-organization alone, nor can one begin to ascertain which of many intervention strategies might be effective in helping solve particular problems. (Elinor Ostrom 1990, 25)

## The Limits of Institutional Design

The focus on positive transaction costs leads us to the third major lesson of institutional economics, which Elinor Ostrom made the focus of her Nobel Prize address (Elinor Ostrom 2010a, see also Elinor Ostrom 2014): *Complex institutions evolve, and, to truly understand them, one needs to focus on the process of their emergence.* A corollary of this is that *efficient institutions are more likely to emerge when self-governance is allowed.* This is because, when all those subjected to the rules are given a voice, on one hand, the opportunism and self-interest of one party is balanced by that of other parties, hence avoiding exploitative institutions, and, on the other hand, the dispersed and personal knowledge that different people might have gets a better chance of being used.

This deep concern with self-governance is Bloomington School's most important guideline to the practice of institutional analysis and development. This idea has its philosophical roots in Vincent Ostrom's analysis of American federalism and his interpretation of the constitutional concerns vividly debated when United States was founded (V. Ostrom 1987, 1991b), as well as in his deep appreciation for the Tocquevillian analysis of democracy (Aligica and Boettke 2009; Aligica 2013). Our theoretical assumptions, which often remain implicit, bring into focus some details while leaving others in the background or even leaving us less equipped to notice them. Vincent Ostrom's political philosophy has provided the Bloomington School a particular set of theoretical glasses that has often given them a strikingly different perspective as compared to prevalent views in political science and public administration (Aligica and Boettke 2009; Aligica 2013). Because of Vincent Ostrom's philosophy, Bloomington School scholars, Elinor Ostrom most prominently, were often able to notice and pay attention to things that many others neglected or superficially dismissed. The skepticism about top-down solutions, and the search for bottom-up self-governing solutions, is one of the main intellectual hallmarks of the Bloomington School. As we follow Elinor Ostrom in her scientific adventures, we will be led to explore different applications of this principle.

As Elinor Ostrom noted, the challenges to design complex institutions in a top-down fashion are generally insurmountable. First, "[g]iven the nonlinearity and complexity of many action situations, it is challenging to predict the precise effect of a change in a particular rule" (Elinor Ostrom 2005a, 239). Second, institutional reforms may often involve changes to more than one single rule. But, "[g]iven the logic of combinatorics, it is not possible to conduct a complete analysis of the expected performance of all the potential rule changes that could be made in an effort to improve outcomes" (Elinor Ostrom 2005a, 243). For these reasons, institutional changes do not occur as a result of a careful and comprehensive analysis—which is literally impossible to conduct. They evolve in a bottom-up fashion. As Elinor Ostrom has noted, one of the pervasive myths in "contemporary policy analysis is the view that organization itself requires *central direction*" (Elinor Ostrom 2005a, 240, emphasis in the original). As a consequence of this myth,

[t]he groups who have actually organized themselves are invisible to those who cannot imagine organization without rules and regulations issued by a central authority.... Instead of central direction, what is needed are policies that enhance the accuracy and reliability of information, that provide

low-cost conflict resolution, and that develop the authority to govern resources at multiple levels. (Elinor Ostrom 2005a, 240)

> International donors and nongovernmental organizations, as well as national governments and charities, have often acted, under the banner of environmental conservation, in a way that has unwittingly destroyed the very social capital—shared relationships, norms, knowledge and understanding—that has been used by resource users to sustain the productivity of natural capital over the ages.... We have yet to adequately recognize how the wide diversity of rules groups have devised through the ages work to protect the resources on which they rely. These institutions are most in jeopardy when central government officials assume that they do not exist (or are not effective) simply because the government has not put them in place. (Elinor Ostrom, interviewed by Aligica 2003)

Furthermore, influenced by Friedrich Hayek, Herbert Simon, and Gerd Gigerenzer, the Bloomington School has placed a great deal of emphasis not just on incentive problems, but also on knowledge limitations. Instead of assuming perfect knowledge and infinite capacity for rational calculation, they had based their institutional analysis on a theory of "bounded rationality" (V. Ostrom 1997, chap. 4; Elinor Ostrom 1998). As Vincent Ostrom (1997, 114–16) put it,

> [m]y sense is that the more innovative contributions to the Public Choice tradition of research have come from contributors who were concerned with a better understanding of basic anomalies, social dilemmas, or paradoxes, rather than with applying a single abstract model of economic reasoning to nonmarket decision making.... The future of Public Choice will be determined by its contributions to the epistemic level of choice in the cultural and social sciences and to the constitution of the epistemic order with which we live and work.

The application of economic reasoning to public choices cannot be advanced very far using the postulates of perfectly informed actors participating in competitive markets operating in unitary states directed by a single center of supreme authority. Equilibrating tendencies under those circumstances are likely to sacrifice market rationality to bureaucratic rationality and both market rationality and bureaucratic rationality to corruption. We need to go back to basics to reconsider the human condition and what it means to be a human being relating to other human beings in the world in which they live.

## THE ROLE OF THE EXPERT

This attitude regarding the limits of institutional design leads to a very different perspective on the role of the expert. Vincent Ostrom's personal example with his involvement in 1955 in helping the drafting of the Natural Resources article of the Alaskan Constitution provides a good way to illustrate the concern with avoiding both expert hubris and problems caused by lack of representation (V. Ostrom 2011). His example showcases the view that the expert is supposed to act as a catalyst of self-governance providing democratic representatives the tools to engage in informed negotiations among themselves, rather than as an arrogant outsider who assumes to know what's best for others.

### Vincent Ostrom's Contribution to the Alaskan Constitution

At first, Vincent Ostrom was hired as a consultant to the constitutional committee[2] and was asked to draft the article on natural resources. However, "he demurred, explaining that the law needed to come from the delegates' own experiences with the physical environment reflect the culture of the peoples of the territory, and speak to their aims as political community" (Barbara Allen comments in V. Ostrom 2011, 38). To this aim, the delegates included a lawyer, a geologist, and a mining engineer, all of them widely knowledgeable of the resource problems in Alaska. As Ostrom put it, "I am a fallible human being who cannot exercise perfect hindsight, nor foresight, nor anticipate all contingencies" (V. Ostrom 2011, 46), and "I did not consider myself to be competently knowledgeable about Alaskan resource problems" (p. 48). This epistemic humility proved essential as it turned out that the problems were often subtle, involving multiple uses of the same land and water resources across the year and by different groups of people. "The problem in legislation, then, is to recognize the right to common use and to facilitate the development of common-property rights and commensurate institutional arrangements to avoid the tragedy of the commons and achieve sustainable development of a renewable resource" (p. 52). To this end, all solutions were imperfect, requiring certain trade-offs between traditional local property rights systems and Anglo-Saxon common law rules.

Moreover, the committee shared Vincent Ostrom's concerns with "balancing the interests in sustainable development among the Aleut,

Eskimo, Alaska Natives, the Eyak, Tlingit, Haida, and Tsimshian, and the Russian, Anglo-American, and European cultures that marked the distinctive history of colonization in the far north of the New World" (V. Ostrom 2011, 39). The background to the convention was the fact that "[t]he people of Alaska...resented the practices of exporting—or plundering—raw materials associated with mining and the threat of federal interests in capturing and exporting another resource, oil" (p. 40). Rather than writing it himself, he led discussions among many stakeholders, who eventually agreed upon a form for the article. As the outcome of this process, "the primary focus of sections on wildlife (including fish) and property rights was to secure capacities for the state of Alaska to have greater control of resources development asserted by the 'people of Alaska'" (p. 41). As such "the general principle of political economy" embodied in the Natural Resources article "is the concept that people who are settlers and share in the positive economic development of the state [land] should also share in the economic rent associated with the commonwealth" (p. 51).

## The Expert as a Catalyst of Self-Governance

This view, that the task of the expert is, first, to learn and understand, and, second, to act as a catalyst of self-governance, rather than as a social planner imposing, more or less subtly, their views upon others, represents one of the main ethical values guiding the Bloomington School. This point of view was also shared with other prominent members of the public choice movement of which Vincent and Elinor Ostrom were among the founding members. James Buchanan has also emphatically argued that

> [t]he role of the social scientist who adopts broadly democratic models of government process...[is] to explain and to understand how people do, in fact, govern *themselves*.... The social function is not of improving anything directly; instead, it is that of explaining behavior of a certain sort which, only remotely and indirectly, can lead to improvements in the political process itself. (Buchanan 1979, 145)

This humanistic ethos can indeed be seen throughout the Ostroms' careers, and it is what has guided their research into how communities discover self-governing solutions. As Vincent Ostrom put it, "the focus of our concern is on *people* and the way they choose to relate to one another rather than on *states* or *governments* as such" (V. Ostrom 2011, 341). The novelty of Elinor Ostrom's work, and the fact that so many experts have previously assumed that people are helplessly trapped in tragedies of the commons, can also be attributed to the fact that much of social science lacks this humanistic ethos, and it is instead driven by a social engineering attitude. As Buchanan (1979, 145) complained, "[m]ost economists, and, I suspect, most political scientists, view government as a potentially benevolent despot, making decisions in the 'general' or the 'public' interest, and they deem it their own social function to advise and counsel this despot on, first, the definition of this general interest, and, second, the means of furthering it." By contrast, the ethos of the Bloomington School focused on self-governance:

> The command of the sovereign is not the only way to achieve an ordered way of life. Most societies, most of the time, have relied upon some combination of command structures and consensual arrangements. If we are to create alternatives to imperial orders, we must grapple with the problem of constituting systems of government that operate with the consent of the governed. (Vincent Ostrom, interviewed by Aligica 2003)

This focus on consent and self-governance can be easily misunderstood. What about other normative criteria such as equality or sustainability? Vincent Ostrom surely agreed with moral pluralism as he argued that, when we act as policy analysts, "[o]ur goals must meet multiple standards of acceptability" and that we should bear in mind both "the requirements of liberty and justice as well as those for economic efficiency" (Aligica 2003). But the point about the focus on consent and self-governance is precisely that it lifts us at a meta-normative level where we can remain agnostic about which values should be given priority. The point is to allow individuals to choose their preferred communities based on their own preferences. Rather than trying to impose our own personal values upon everyone, the focus, instead, is on enabling people's capacities to build communities that best fit *their* priorities.

Recently, there has been a significant push against this social engineering attitude, especially in development economics (Easterly 2002, 2007, 2015; Coyne 2013), with Elinor Ostrom's work undoubtedly playing an important role in paving the way. When asked in her Nobel

Prize interview about "people getting involved in their own governance," she answered: "That's what I've been working on for all my life! Humans have great capabilities and somehow we've had some sense that the officials had genetic capabilities that the rest of us didn't have.... I hope we can change that" (Smith 2009).

## NOTES

1. Some of Ronald Coase's (1937) and Oliver Williamson's (1975, 1992, 1996) most important contributions were to explain that firms emerge as a way to address the uncertainties involved in dealing with suppliers of inputs. Coase showed that firms and organizations exist because finding partners on the market sometimes takes too much time and effort. Williamson showed that firms grow, integrating several different areas of activity in a single organization, as a way of avoiding the uncertainties created by the possibility of opportunistic behavior.

2. Properly establishing a constitutional Resources Committee was also crucial, because, in order to satisfy the ideal of self-governance, all relevant stakeholders needed to be included and informed. This task was organized by the "architect" of the Alaskan Constitution, Thomas B. Stewart, and several civil society organizations contributed in the "preconvention" step promoting discussions and informing the general public.

# Chapter One

# Against Gargantua

## The Study of Local Public Economies

The presumption that economies of scale were prevalent was wrong; the presumption that you needed a single police department was wrong; and the presumption that individual departments wouldn't be smart enough to work out ways of coordinating is wrong.... For patrolling, if you don't know the neighborhood, you can't spot the early signs of problems, and if you have five or six layers of supervision, the police chief doesn't know what's occurring on the street.

(Elinor Ostrom, interviewed by Zagorski 2006)

I have seen the ways that police officers serving an independent community, where local citizens have constituted it, deal with citizens. Citizens are treated differently when you live in a central city served by a metropolitan police department. Many of the officers in very big departments do not see themselves as responsible to citizens. They are on duty for specific hours and with an entirely different mentality.... When you are in a police car for eight hours with officers from a big department, you learn that they really do not know the area they are currently serving since they rotate so frequently. When I was in a police car with an officer from a moderately sized department, they would start telling me about the local community, where there are trouble spots, and where few problems occur. They watch trouble spots that they see potentially emerging. They would sometimes take a juvenile to their home in order to discuss problems they are observing. They do not put kids in jail the first time they observe behavior that is problematic. In the big cities, officers tend to charge juveniles who have been seen to commit small offenses right away. Many jails are overcrowded with juveniles in large cities. Problems of

*Photo 2.  Elinor Ostrom (center), Roger Parks (left), and Diane Eubanks (right)
Analyze Data on American Law Enforcement Agencies ("A Panel Discussion:
Dr. James Buchanan's Contributions to Social Philosophy and
Political Economy," Mercatus Center, 2010).*

law enforcement in central urban districts have grown over time and are
linked to the way urban governance has been shifted to ever-larger units.
(Elinor Ostrom, cited by Boettke, Palagashvili, and Lemke 2013)

The first big impact that Elinor Ostrom and her team have had was
thanks to their empirical study of local public economies. To the extent
that people follow politics, it is usually the national-level politics that
captures their attention. But, in many ways, the local level has a more
direct impact upon our lives. The local-level issues tend to gather our
attention mainly when something goes terribly wrong: police brutality
in Ferguson, Missouri; poisoned drinking water in Flint, Michigan;
the George Washington Bridge lane closure scandal in Fort Lee, New
Jersey; the failure of public schools in Philadelphia; and so on. In many
ways we don't usually hear that much about local public economies
because, by comparison to national-level policies, things actually tend
to work much better. The Bloomington School's work on local public
economies helps explain why the local public sector usually works

relatively well as well as why the failures that we observe have a specific pattern. When local politics fails, it does not fail at random. The failure is usually a failure of scale: either due to an unfortunate top-down intrusion upon the local level or due to the inability of local communities to overcome the transaction costs involved in cooperating for producing larger-scale collective goods. In the relatively distant past, the second type of problem was much more prevalent than it is today. Historically, the emergence of the nation state acted as a means to solve the problems caused by over-decentralization. Nowadays, however, it is the top-down intrusion that usually causes most problems, which is why the Bloomington School, and this book, focuses more on it.

## FROM UCLA TO INDIANA

The opening salvo of Bloomington School's foray into the study of local public economies was a theoretical article written by Vincent Ostrom, Charles Tiebout, and Robert Warren in 1961, titled "The organization of government in metropolitan areas" (also included in McGinnis 1999b, chap. 1; and in V. Ostrom 1991b, chap. 6). This work was supported by the Bureau of Governmental Research at UCLA, the Haynes Foundation, and by the Water Resources Center of the University of California, but they were far from happy with the result. In fact, they had wanted the exact opposite conclusion. It was very common at the time to think that the consolidation of local administrations into larger centralized administrative units would increase efficiency, due to economies of scale and the elimination of overlapping efforts, as argued for instance by Anderson and Weidner's book *American City Government* (1950). They were hoping for a study that would provide more academic support to these calls to centralize the administration in metropolitan areas. More specifically, they wanted something that supported the "Lakewood Plan":

> Ostrom was already interested by the implications of the 1954 incorporation of the city of Lakewood, California... which, in an unprecedented political bargain, would contract out the majority of its municipal services with Los Angeles County. The "Lakewood Plan," as it came to be called, quickly became the model for succeeding contract cities in Los Angeles and nationwide. (Singleton 2015)

But, instead of going along with the fashionable view at the time, Ostrom, Tiebout, and Warren wrote a powerful defense of the benefits of decentralization and overlapping jurisdictions. Their intent was to use economic theory as a tool

> for escaping political scientists' "compulsion to want to superimpose a structure in such political situation[s]." As the research plan explained, in contrast with the political scientist: "The economist might apply a model of industrial organization and treat the interaction within the area as the operation of the market system, recognizing the existence of imperfect competition in an oligopolistic setting." ... [Ostrom and Tiebout] sought to place the organization of metropolitan governments in an explicitly economic framework, where municipal services were bought and sold in a "quasimarket." This theorizing, however, drew the ire of other political scientists in the bureau, resulting in Tiebout's and Ostrom's removal from the project and the eventual joint authorship of an article with Robert Warren instead. (Singleton 2015)

To make matters worse from the point of view of the consolidationists, the article got published by the *American Political Science Review*, the top political science journal in the world, and became massively cited. Referring to the consolidationists as supporters of "Gargantua" probably didn't help win them many favors either. The conflict with UCLA's Bureau of Governmental Research eventually led both Vincent Ostrom and Charles Tiebout to leave the university. Their initial intention was to go beyond just theory, but the conflict with the bureau prevented it:

> The Lakewood Project—the study of the contract system in Los Angeles—will be approached in light of the model furnished by economics. Rather than as a limited examination of relations between political units, this study will evaluate the performance of the county government as a seller of goods and services, and of particular local units as the buyers of these services, as unions organized to meet the demand of consumers (the citizens). ("An Approach to Metropolitan Areas," Research Seminar Minutes, September 23, 1959, UCLA's Bureau of Governmental Research, cited by Singleton 2015)

This empirical program will be revived in the 1970s by Elinor Ostrom and her students. On the theoretical side, "[Vincent] Ostrom wanted to adapt the Lakewood project research into a book, titled 'A New Approach to the Study of Metropolitan Government' ... though it never materialized" (Singleton 2015). He did, however, develop the polycentricity concept further (V. Ostrom 1972, 1991a). Robert Warren finished his dissertation under Vincent Ostrom and published some of the Lakewood project findings together with his theoretical analysis (1966). Historically, metropolitan areas emerged in an unplanned fashion as small towns gradually grew up to the point where they reached one another, and combined into one de facto, but not *de jure*, large urban area. The administrative organization of these metropolitan areas remained decentralized because of their history. The question was: Should they now be centralized under a larger hierarchical system? The de facto organization was "polycentric" reflecting the "multiplicity of political jurisdictions in a metropolitan area" (V. Ostrom, Tiebout, and Warren 1961). Should this be changed? Polycentricity became an important concept, and it was the topic of Elinor Ostrom's Nobel Prize address (2010a) because it not only merely describes the de facto situation, but can also be used to understand why the system works relatively well, in the sense that it has desirable *emergent, unplanned properties.*

Polycentricity was first defined as a system of "many centers of decision making that are formally independent of each other" (V. Ostrom, Tiebout, and Warren 1961), but which, nonetheless, are forced to interact in both competitive and cooperative fashions, and may be embedded into larger systems: the decision centers "take each other into account in competitive undertakings or have recourse to central mechanisms to resolve conflicts," and, as a result, "the various political jurisdictions in a metropolitan area may function in a coherent manner with consistent and predictable patterns of interacting behavior" (V. Ostrom, Tiebout, and Warren 1961).

Once they moved to Indiana University and started the workshop, they were able to return to the initial idea. Initially, Elinor Ostrom was hired for teaching "Introduction to American Government" on Tuesdays, Thursdays, and Saturdays at 7:30 a.m. "How could I say no?" she joked later (Zagorski 2006). But the position eventually changed to a tenured one, and when she started having PhD students in the 1970s, she told them to pick up any empirical topic except groundwater, as she was tired of that subject after having done her dissertation on it (this was only temporary). At the suggestion of Roger Parks, they chose to study police departments. This was not an entirely foreign subject to Elinor Ostrom. As a graduate student, she had been a part of Robert Warren's team in Vincent's Lakewood Project.

Building on Ostrom, Tiebout, and Warren's theoretical article and on the initial idea behind the Lakewood Project, a large number of empirical studies followed (Bish 1971; Bish and Kirk 1974; Elinor Ostrom 1976b; Elinor Ostrom, Parks, and Whitaker 1978; Bish and Ostrom 1979; V. Ostrom, Bish, and Ostrom 1988; McGinnis 1999b; see also Aligica and Boettke 2009 for more on the social philosophy behind these studies). As Roger Parks recalls (included in McGinnis 1999b, 349),

> In the spring of 1970, an intrepid band of graduate and undergraduate students, ably led by Lin Ostrom, set forth on the streets of Indianapolis and its close suburbs. Their task was to collect data relevant to the question of whether police services were better supplied by large, highly professionalized bureaus or by much smaller departments characteristic of most suburban United States. In the face of recent [then] and recurring recommendations for consolidation of police forces, other public services, and local governments in urban areas, this venture seemed quixotic, but it was instead quite productive. From it sprang a stream of Workshop research that kept many of our friends employed. This research, we believe, helped to change the tenor of debates over how to organize policing in urban areas and, more broadly, whether consolidation of local governments in metropolitan areas was the unmixed blessing perceived by its proponents.

Perhaps we get the clearest idea as to why these studies were so successful from Elinor Ostrom's 1972 article, "Metropolitan Reform: Propositions Derived from Two Traditions" (included in McGinnis 1999b, chap. 6). This article draws a series of empirically testable hypotheses about the efficiency of local public services from, on one hand, the consolidationist perspective and from, on the other hand, the "political economy" perspective of V. Ostrom, Tiebout, and Warren and the other public choice scholars (such as George Stigler,[1] Mancur Olson,[2] William Niskanen,[3] and Wallace Oates[4]), and then moves toward testing them empirically. The two perspectives are, hence, turned from being two grand conflicting *philosophical* visions to being simply two sets of hypotheses about how the world works, ready for scientific testing. Furthermore, as I discuss in more detail in Chapter 2, the challenge of actually testing these hypotheses has shined a bright light upon the conceptual difficulties of trying to assess the quality of public services, and of evaluating what an "optimal" tradeoff between quality and cost might be (V. Ostrom and Ostrom 1977).

This approach, taking apart what may appear as high-level philo-sophical musings into their elementary components with the purpose of deriving empirically testable hypotheses, was one of the staples of Vincent Ostrom's teaching. Filippo Sabetti, a graduate student at the workshop in the late 1960s to the early 1970s, who became a promi-nent first-generation "Workshopper," recalls that Vincent Ostrom's graduate course "was based on readings derived largely from classical texts on America and the first generation of public choice scholars" (Sabetti 2011), covering books such as *The Federalist*, Tocqueville's *Democracy in America*, Hobbes' *Leviathan*, Buchanan and Tullock's *The Calculus of Consent*, and Olson's *The Logic of Collective Action*. But Vincent Ostrom had a rather unusual approach to guiding students through these texts. His approach was "to pursue the logic of the propo-sitions as testable hypotheses (at least by experience if not by rigorous field research)" (Sabetti 2011).

We can see the success of the Bloomington School as emerging from this challenging approach to teaching that Vincent Ostrom employed, which was followed and expanded by Elinor Ostrom: "By early 1970s Lin's courses applying the Workshop's theoretical conceptions in rigor-ous fieldwork of police studies as well as in other modes of quantitative analysis and modeling, including game theory, had become part of the core curriculum, complementing Vincent's 'macro theoretic' approach with empirical studies and 'micro theory'" (Sabetti 2011). What made Vincent and Elinor Ostrom such successful intellectual and academic entrepreneurs, was not just that they had spotted neglected opportunities for research, but also that they developed their teaching curriculum and style to complement the research agenda.

It is perhaps worth pointing out that this approach to teaching stems from a particular philosophy of language, most prominently associated with John Searle and Michael Devitt (Searle 1969, 1999; Devitt and Sterelny 1999; see also Carnap 1950). Vincent Ostrom was particularly fond of Searle's (1969) *Speech Acts*. One of the key questions in the philosophy of language is "What is meaning?" To put it differently, when can we say that we truly understand some-thing? Philosophers like Searle and Devitt argue that the meaning of a text (be it a single sentence or a larger text) is nothing but the set of empirical conditions that would have to hold in the real world for us to accept that what the text is saying is indeed true. In other words, to understand the meaning of a text, you have to be able to identify the ways in which the world would be different depending on whether the text were true or false.

As you can imagine, if this is your theory of language, you would indeed want to teach like Vincent Ostrom. As a professor, you would not believe that your students have truly understood a reading, be it as philosophical as it may be, unless they are able to derive empirically testable hypotheses from it. In turn, this has the great benefit of implicitly preparing the students to be empirical scientists who might be able to tackle problems that many others would find too daunting. After all, once you've been forced to try to find testable hypotheses out of abstract philosophical texts, you may find it relatively easier to think empirically about more mundane scientific questions. Undoubtedly, Elinor Ostrom herself was one of the greatest students of this method, and what makes the Bloomington School rather unusual is that it successfully spans across the entire continuum from very high-minded social and political philosophy all the way to the most hard-nosed empiricism.

## THE COMPLEXITY OF PUBLIC SERVICES

The provision of safety and protection is the most basic of governmental services. How should police departments be organized to provide the best services at the lowest cost? Elinor Ostrom coordinated a series of field studies of police services starting in Indianapolis, Chicago, Grand Rapids, Nashville–Davidson Country and St. Louis, followed by a much more extensive national-level study covering 80 out of the 200 Standard Metropolitan Statistical Areas (SMSAs). This is still the largest study of police departments ever performed. As already mentioned, at the time, there were numerous calls to reform the organization of police departments by consolidating them. However, they discovered that "[n]one of the major national recommendations for change cite empirical evidence to support their contentions," and, furthermore, they were based on large misconceptions about how police departments were actually organized (Elinor Ostrom, Parks, and Whitaker 1978, xxii). To make matters worse, the only areas that had been "frequently studied by national commissions, state and federal agencies, and social scientists" were the "[p]olice departments in the very large metropolitan areas," despite "nearly half the nation's people living outside the 16 largest metropolitan areas"

(Elinor Ostrom, Parks, and Whitaker 1978, 7–8). Consequently, the recommendations for police "reform" were not just done *without* accurate information, but they were actually based on misleading and nonrepresentative information gathered only from the largest metropolitan areas:

> The New York City Police Department, the Chicago Police Department, the Los Angeles Police Department, and similar large city police agencies have been studied extensively. They are the models used explicitly or implicitly in judging other police departments across the country. But little has been written about the ways in which smaller police agencies work in relation to each other in small- and medium-sized urban areas across the country. (Elinor Ostrom, Parks, and Whitaker 1978, 2)

Furthermore,

> Many observers have expressed concern about the existence of small departments. In their opinion these agencies cannot possibly provide the wide range of services offered by large central city police departments. Major changes in the law enforcement systems of metropolitan areas have been proposed. These changes are being considered without much information (other than the number and size distribution of agencies) about how services are delivered. (Elinor Ostrom, Parks, and Whitaker 1978, 2)

In response to this challenge, Elinor Ostrom and her collaborators sought, first, to understand how these smaller police departments actually work, and, second, to evaluate how well they are doing their job. They analyzed three types of "direct services"—patrol, traffic control, and criminal investigation—and four types of "auxiliary services"— radio communication, adult pretrial detention, entry-level training, and crime labs. While the direct services impact citizens directly, the auxiliary services are factors of production used by the direct services. What they found was precisely what V. Ostrom, Tiebout, and Warren (1961) have intuited: such different services often have different optimal scales of production, and the organization of police departments involves complex delivery patterns, involving (1) autonomous local provision of some services, (2) cooperation between jurisdictions for larger scale problems, (3) alternate provision, based on predefined criteria, of the same service by more than one agency in the same jurisdiction, (4) only very rarely, duplication of the service provision by more than one agency without either cooperation or predefined criteria for alternation. As an example of these complex patterns of delivery, consider their in-depth analysis of the Cumberland County in North Carolina, the location of the Fayetteville metropolitan area (Figure 1.1). In this county, several jurisdictions are present: the military base at Fort Bragg, the Pope Air Force Base, Hope Mills, Spring Lake, Fayetteville, Fayetteville State University, and the rest of the county.

With respect to patrol services, each of these areas has its own patrol, with the exception of the unincorporated part of the county, roughly covering everything east of I-95, which is patrolled by the North Carolina Highway Patrol.

The situation is much different with respect to homicides investigations. Criminal investigations in Fort Bragg and in Pope Air Force Base "alternate" between the Federal Bureau of Investigations and the U.S. Army Criminal Investigations Division or U.S. Air Force Office of Special Investigations, depending on whether the homicides

Figure 1.1.   Cumberland County, NC.

involve civilians or only military personnel (Elinor Ostrom, Parks, and Whitaker 1978, 42–44). In Hope Mills and Spring Lake, the local police department cooperates with the Cumberland County Sheriff's Department. In Fayetteville, including the university, the city's police department has sole jurisdiction, while the rest of the county is serviced by the sheriff.

The auxiliary services also showcase interesting examples of complex patterns of delivery (Elinor Ostrom, Parks, and Whitaker 1974, 1978, 50). For instance, the entry-level training is provided internally in the cases of the U.S. Army Military Police, the U.S. Air Force Security Police, the U.S. Air Force Office of Special Investigations, the FBI, the North Carolina Highway Patrol, and the North Carolina State Bureau of Investigations. By contrast, the Fayetteville Technical Institute is providing entry-level training for the police departments in Hope Mills, Spring Lake, Fayetteville, Fayetteville State University, and Cumberland County Sherriff's Department. Interestingly, the Spring Lake Police Department also gets some of its training from the Johnston Technical Institute—an example of duplication of services. But the competition between technical institutes is probably beneficial for keeping the quality of the training high.

In the case of crime labs, while the Fort Bragg and the Pope Air Force Base have their own labs, the police departments in Fayetteville, Spring Lake, Hope Mills, and the rest of the Cumberland County use either the Fayetteville–Cumberland County Crime Lab or the NC Bureau of Investigation Lab, the two labs cooperating with each other (Elinor Ostrom, Parks, and Whitaker 1974, also included in McGinnis 1999b, chap. 11).

Similarly, in the case of adult pretrial detention, the following arrangement exists among three producers:

> The county sheriff provides adult detention facilities for all local police units. Each of the two military installations maintains its own detention facility. Military personnel taken into custody by civilian departments are usually remanded to their base for detention. Civilians arrested on one of the military bases would be sent to the county jail for detention. Thus, the three producers can be viewed as alternative services restricted by clientele. (Elinor Ostrom, Parks, and Whitaker 1974)

This kind of analysis for one metropolitan area was replicated to all 80 metropolitan areas with similar results about complexity and cooperation across agencies. For example, although many police departments have their own crime labs, "[s]tate agencies supply lab services to police agencies in all but 1 of 80 SMSAs. Seven states (California, Connecticut, Kentucky, Massachusetts, Oklahoma, Ohio, and South Carolina) have two different state agencies that supply lab services to direct service police agencies" (Elinor Ostrom, Parks, and Whitaker 1978, 279). The bottom line is that, despite the conventional wisdom at the time that "having all services within the same department facilitates communication and coordination ... in studying SMSAs with extensive division of services across agencies, we have, however, found considerable interdepartmental communication and coordination" (Elinor Ostrom, Parks, and Whitaker 1978, xxxv). In other words, one of the main arguments of consolidationists was shown to be based on a very poorly informed perspective about how metropolitan areas actually operate. The consolidationists held that

> [f]ragmentation of police services is extreme.... Wasted energies are lost motion due to overlapping, duplication, and noncooperation are not the worst consequences of this fragmentation. Large areas of the United States—particularly rural communities and the small jurisdictions in or near metropolitan areas—lack anything resembling modern, professional police protection. (Committee for Economic Development, cited by Elinor Ostrom, Parks, and Whitaker 1974)

This was certainly *not* what Elinor Ostrom and her collaborators found to be the case. The consolidationists turned out to be mainly engaged in scare tactics and preconceived ideas with virtually no grounding in reality. The reality on the ground, as described above, was much better characterized as "polycentric":

> By "polycentric" I mean a system where citizens are able to organize not just one but multiple governing authorities, as well as private arrangements, at different scales. Each unit may exercise considerable independence to make and enforce rules within a circumscribed scope of authority for a specified geographical area. In a polycentric system, some units are general-purpose governments, whereas others may be highly specialized [such as] ... special districts, private associations, or parts of local government. These are nested in several levels of general-purpose governments that also provide civil equity as well as criminal courts. (Elinor Ostrom, interviewed by Aligica 2003)

**Table 1.1.** Performance of Consolidated versus Independent Police
Departments

| Variables | Independent Communities | Indianapolis Neighborhoods |
|---|---|---|
| *Experience variables* | | |
| Victimization | + | − |
| Willingness to report victimization | + | − |
| Extent of police follow-up | + | − |
| Assistance | + | − |
| Promptness of response | + | − |
| Quality of assistance | = | = |
| Stopped as suspected offender | = | = |
| *Evaluation variables* | | |
| Promptness | + | − |
| Crime trend | + | − |
| Potential for bribe taking | = | = |
| Police–citizens relations | + | − |
| General evaluation of job being done | + | − |

*Legend*: + means a higher level of performance, − means a lower level of performance, and = means similar level of performance.

*Source*: E. Ostrom and Whitaker (1973), chap. 8 in McGinnis (1999b, 197).

This type of a polycentric organization is not restricted solely to police departments. It covers *all* aspects of public economies. As we'll see later in the chapter, we should expect, for a number of reasons, that *any* hierarchical arrangement of public economies will unavoidably be inefficient and slow to respond to changes, and the only way to have a responsive system is to have a polycentric system which addresses various issues at different scales. This means that, to the extent that our governments are democratically accountable, we should expect them to create a polycentric organization of public administration. To the extent that politicians and other "public entrepreneurs" face constraints in having to deliver good governance, they will be guided by the inherent logic of the complexity of collective goods to create polycentric arrangements. It is thus not an accident that we observe polycentric systems everywhere across the world where self-governance is allowed to operate as a guiding principle.

Ignoring polycentricity, partly because of misguided ideas about "reform," can potentially generate huge costs, especially due to the logic of bureaucracy which makes it exceedingly difficult to turn back from such "reforms" later, once they have failed. Elinor Ostrom begins her introduction to *The Delivery of Urban Services* by highlighting this very issue: "Failure, in many cases, leads to adoption of another program—one often based, as was the first, on inadequate analysis of the strategic behavior of the different actors. Failure seems to breed failure" (Elinor Ostrom 1976b, 7).

## THE RISE AND FALL OF COMMUNITY POLICING

What about the quality of police protection? As Elinor Ostrom (2010b) recalled, after comparing "police departments serving similar neighborhoods within a metropolitan area ... [w]e never found a large department policing numerous neighborhoods that outperformed smaller departments within the same metropolitan area in regard to direct services to citizens." Furthermore, the "most efficient producers supply more output for given inputs in high multiplicity metropolitan areas than do the efficient producers in metropolitan areas with fewer producers" (E. Ostrom and Parks 1987, chap. 12 in McGinnis 1999b, 287).

The task of measuring the performance of different police departments was a challenge in itself:

> When conducting studies in the Indianapolis, Chicago, St. Louis, Rochester, and Tampa–St. Petersburg metropolitan areas, we solved the severe problem of measuring police performance by collecting performance data from interviews with a random sample of households served by small and large departments. Information was obtained about victimization, willingness to call the police, speed of police response, amount of police follow-up, satisfaction levels with police contacts, and general evaluations of the quality of policing in a neighborhood. (Elinor Ostrom 2000)

After comparing similar neighborhoods, the conclusion was entirely at odds with the received "wisdom" of consolidation:

> The consistent finding from this series of studies is that small and medium-sized police departments perform more effectively than large police departments serving similar neighborhoods, and frequently at lower costs.... Victimization rates tend to be lower, police response tends to be faster, citizens tend to be more willing to call on police, citizens tend to more positively evaluate specific contacts with the police, and citizens tend to rate police higher across a series of other evaluative questions. Further, citizens living in small communities tend to be more informed about how to change local policies, tend to know more policemen serving their neighborhoods, and call the police more frequently to obtain general information than do citizens living in large cities. Citizens served by small departments tend to receive better services at lower costs than their neighbors living in the center city. Instead of being a "problem" for the metropolitan area, small departments frequently contribute to the improvement of police services in the area. (Elinor Ostrom 2000).

Figure 1.2 Citizens' satisfaction survey ranging from "Outstanding" to "Inadequate" (Source of data: Parks 1995, chap. 15 in McGinnis 1999b, 350) show a comparison of the satisfaction with police performance

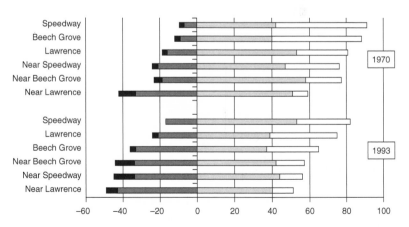

**Figure 1.2. Performance of Independent versus Consolidated Police Departments.**

between six neighborhoods in the Indianapolis area (E. Ostrom and Whitaker 1973 and Parks 1995, cited in chaps. 8 and 15, respectively, in McGinnis 1999b). Beech Grove, Lawrence, and Speedway have independent small-scale police departments, while the nearby neighborhoods are part of the Indianapolis consolidated police. We see that across the board, the satisfaction with the police is greater in the smaller departments—indicative of the fact that smaller departments tend to be more responsive to citizens' needs. We also see that, across the board, the satisfaction with the police departments has decreased from 1970 to 1993, but it has decreased more in the consolidated departments.

## How Reliable Are Citizens' Surveys?

At first, they received some pushback on their findings due to skepticism about using surveys:

> Many scholars and public officials are uneasy about any reliance upon data collected from a survey of citizens about public agency performance. Citizens are thought by some to be uninformed and unable to give reliable perceptions and/or evaluations of service levels. Whether one agrees with this view or not (we obviously do not), reliance upon any single mode of measurement can lead to errors or biases in measuring performance or productivity. (Elinor Ostrom 1976a)

In a sense, the anti-self-governance bias is so strong that many experts would even deny that people know more about their local conditions than the remote experts.

To counteract this line of criticism, they designed other experiments comparing objective measures of roads and street lighting with citizens' perceptions. Street lighting was somewhat straightforward to measure using a precision light-meter. With respect to roads, they have used a so-called rough-o-meter developed by the Urban Institute, which basically amounted to measuring how smooth it is to drive a car on a road. This was basically an early version of the "Street Bump" smart phone app that exists today, which uses people's phones to detect bumps in the road as they're driving, and which is now used by some city governments to collect information about potholes. They have also "developed an observation form and procedure which can be used by trained observers to record specific data about various aspects of street condition ... [including] among other items, measuring all potholes on a

blockface with a 'yardstick pothole measurer'" (Elinor Ostrom 1976a).
Elinor Ostrom recalled how:

> On Palm Sunday one year ago, I found myself walking down an
> Indianapolis street, carrying a yardstick and dashing out between pass-
> ing cars to measure potholes in the street. Why would any sane person
> dash out onto a busy street to risk their life to measure some holes in the
> ground? I must confess that I asked myself that question several times that
> day and other days while I helped develop out "unobtrusive" measures of
> road conditions. (Elinor Ostrom 1976a)

The bottom line is that the comparison between objective physical measures and subjective perceptions revealed a high degree of correlation,
contrary to the critics who "assumed inaccuracy of citizen perceptions of
service levels." Some differences existed between people, with "persons
with more than a high school diploma, those over 45, those who have
lived on a block more than five years, and those living on medium to
short blocks tended to be more 'accurate' in their perceptions of road
roughness" (Elinor Ostrom 1976a). Interestingly, the only perception
flaw they could find was that citizens' misjudgment of the lighting conditions over the entire street was found to be similar to those in close
proximity to their own homes . The study basically established that citizens' perceptions were far more reliable than the critics were suggesting.

Turning again to the issue of evaluating police services, they noted
that apparently more objective indicators are actually deeply flawed.
Most police departments evaluate themselves by looking at *inputs*,
rather than at outputs. "The internal records of most police departments consist mainly on workload data: rates of reported crime, traffic
citations, and clearance of reported cases, for example.... Consumers'
evaluations of the services they are receiving are not recorded at any
point in routine police records" (E. Ostrom and Whitaker 1973, cited in
chap. 8 in McGinnis 1999b, 180).

## The Failure of "Community Policing"

Partly as a result of these police and local public economies studies, a
reform movement took shape in the 1980s. The calls for a move toward
"community policing" became more popular. As a result of this,

> [p]olice departments were advised to put police officers and commu-
> nity members in closer proximity by creating police "substations" and

requiring police departments to have officers on foot patrol. These changes were intended to modify the existing conception of police as outsiders or threats and give better ground for community–police relationships. Another popular action was to hold community–police meetings so that the community could meet the officers and the officers could better understand the needs of the community. (Boettke, Lemke, and Palagashvili 2015)

At first glance, such reforms should have worked. But, instead, the results are generally mixed or negative, and the "reduction in crime [has been] primarily due to a trend towards larger police forces that has little to do with the adoption of any particular policing strategy" (Boettke, Lemke, and Palagashvili 2015). These moves toward "community policing" have been, however, largely illusory or superficial. Part of the problem is that "community policing" has been adopted as a top-down policy and in many ways has been a form without content— more of a populist slogan than a genuine reform. A bigger part of the problem is that police activities have actually been centralized, with a greater impact of the federal level on local police departments, especially due to the War on Drugs and due to moves toward police militarization. In other words, whatever moves toward genuine community policing have been made, they have been swamped by further centralization:

> The top-down approach to the establishment of community policing and the increasing reach of federal interventions into local law enforcement have prevented the emergence of true community policing as understood by Ostrom and her colleagues at The Workshop. Instead there has been a trend towards centralization and militarization of the police, shifting the focus away from the needs of the community and towards the homogenous goals of federal policy. (Boettke, Lemke, and Palagashvili 2012)

To make matters worse, the police–community meetings have gradually been bureaucratized, and as "the city began to send fewer beat police and more bureaucrats to community meetings … participation waned as citizens began to feel that the purpose of the meetings had shifted from learning about citizen concerns to persuading the community to support traditional police action" (Boettke, Lemke, and Palagashvili 2015). This failure of "community policing" was not so surprising to the Bloomington School itself. In fact Elinor Ostrom had warned precisely of this possible distortion of the idea right from the beginning. She noted that,

> [t]he problems in obtaining an adequate knowledge about local situations have led several large-scale police departments to experiment with local commander systems and other arrangements to decentralize administrative control of neighborhood patrol forces. While this reform may increase direct supervision of patrolmen in the field and may lead to more effective coordination of their efforts within neighborhoods, *it may be expected to decrease the responsiveness to citizens of patrolmen serving these areas*. (E. Ostrom and Whitaker 1974, chap. 9 in McGinnis 1999b, 225, emphasis added)

In other words, community policing when properly understood involves not just a decentralized mechanism for knowledge aggregation, but also—and this is critically important—allowing the *goals* of the local government to be determined by the local citizens. A decentralized police agency that takes orders from the federal government, and that is dependent on the central government for revenues and equipment, is not going to be responsive to citizens' needs, and, hence, will not perform well in terms of most criteria of citizens' satisfaction.

The idea that local police departments should be financially independent of central government, and, in order to be responsive to citizens, should be paid by the local community is known as "fiscal equivalence" (Buchanan and Tullock 1962, 292–93; Olson 1969; V. Ostrom and Ostrom 1977). This was already familiar to Elinor Ostrom and her collaborators, and they recognized its importance in connection to the problem of political representation:

> Local control of the police would involve the establishment of formal structures of accountability to the public being served [rather than to the central government] as well as indirect internal supervision of patrolmen on the job. An effective means of establishing local control of the police in large cities might be to set up neighborhood districts to handle a variety of *locally confined public problems*. Such units would require some means of public selection of officials and *the authority to levy local taxes* and establish local ordinances. (E. Ostrom and Whitaker 1974, chap. 9 in McGinnis 1999b, 225, emphasis added)

The idea of fiscal equivalence is usually controversial because it implies that rich neighborhoods will have more resources than poor ones, and, hence better services. Elinor Ostrom's response to this is two-fold. On one hand, centralizing police departments and other local public services will not lead to improved outcomes for the poor neighborhoods; on the contrary, it further robs them of political representation. Centralized governments still respond more to richer constituencies, and, hence, absent local political representation, poorer neighborhoods will be even more likely to be left behind.

On the other hand, she notes that redistribution can be, to some extent, pursued as a distinct activity. We don't need to centralize the entire local public economy, with all its activities, just to distribute money to poorer neighborhoods. This being said, in order to avoid the Samaritan's Dilemma—the perverse distortion of the aid recipients' incentives away from self-reliance—she argued that redistribution should be kept limited to emergency situations: "Citywide forces could be utilized to supplement the needs of any local area *in times of emergency*. Redistribution to the poorer neighborhood districts within the large city could be provided from citywide as well as state and federal sources" (E. Ostrom and Whitaker 1974, chap. 9 in McGinnis 1999b, 225, emphasis added).

It is also important to bear in mind that performance depends to a large extent on *how* the money is spent, rather than on *how much* is spent. For instance, they have found that "Chicago police spent 14 times the dollar amount that the independent police departments did—but despite this differential in expenditure, citizens in the smaller communities received the same or higher level of service" (Boettke, Palagashvili, and Lemke 2013).

This type of problem is most evident with respect to black neighborhoods. The study of police departments in Chicago found that "[b]lack citizens are among the constituents cited as least satisfied with the performance of local police and other public officials." Redistribution did not help. On the contrary,

[r]edistribution of resources, itself, is not sufficient to bring about responsive police services. It appears that considerable resource redistribution is currently occurring within the city of Chicago. More resources are probably devoted to policing in black neighborhoods studied than are in derived revenue for such purposes from these areas. Residents of these neighborhoods, however, find police services no better and police somewhat less responsive than do village residents *despite* the much greater

difference in resources devoted to policing. (E. Ostrom and Whitaker 1974, chap. 9 in McGinnis 1999b, 224)

They have found that because of so-called preventive policing, there was, paradoxically, both too much policing and too little, as "police forces simultaneously increase the resentment of residents and divert manpower from other activities such as answering calls and investigating the many crimes that do occur in the ghetto" (E. Ostrom and Whitaker 1974, chap. 9 in McGinnis 1999b, 207). Interestingly, the negative attitudes of black citizens toward the police were inversely related to their income: "black respondents of higher income levels tended to be less likely to give high ratings to police than black respondents of lower income levels" (E. Ostrom and Whitaker 1974, chap. 9 in McGinnis 1999b, 206). The bottom line is that in Chicago, as well as in other cities, "[p]olice seems to be failing to serve residents of many black neighborhoods in US cities" (E. Ostrom and Whitaker 1974, chap. 9 in McGinnis 1999b, 207), and the main reason is the subversion of genuinely local public economies by top-down control.

Since the Bloomington School did these studies, the situation seems to have deteriorated. For example, in Chicago today, a recent study by the Chicago Police Accountability Task Force, with members appointed by Mayor Rahm Emanuel, has revealed a shocking situation (Lopez 2016). The report found that black residents were far more likely to be"[s]topped without justification, verbally and physically abused, and in some instances arrested, and then detained without counsel." Furthermore, out of "404 police shootings between 2008 and 2015 ... [a]mong the victims, 74 percent were black, even though black people make up just 33 percent of Chicago's population. ... Of the 1,886 Taser uses between 2012 and 2015, 76 percent of those hit by stun guns were black." This decades-long history of police racism significantly worsened due to the War on Drugs and police militarization (Boettke, Lemke, and Palagashvili 2012, 2015; Coyne and Hall-Blanco 2016), and it is now even more difficult to change: "False arrests, coerced confessions and wrongful convictions are also a part of this history. Lives lost and countless more damaged. These events and others mark a long, sad history of death, false imprisonment, physical and verbal abuse and general discontent about police actions in neighborhoods of color" (Lopez 2016).

Back in 1974, Elinor Ostrom and Gordon Whitaker analyzed a variety of reform proposals, including calls for the increased "professionalization of the police force" and access to larger funding. Their conclusion was that "[p]olice effectiveness depends, in part, on police understanding the nature of the community being served and police openness to suggestions, criticism, and complaints" (E. Ostrom and Whitaker 1974, chap. 9 in McGinnis 1999b, 224). As a result, "[c]ommunity control of police may, thus, provide an institutional framework for the effective expression of black citizen demands for impartial police service.... Professionalism alone does not appear to provide sufficient controls so that police will be responsive to their needs for protection and respect. Community control places that responsibility on the people themselves and provides them with the mechanisms by which to exercise it" (E. Ostrom and Whitaker 1974, chap. 9 in McGinnis 1999b, 225–26). Unfortunately, this advice was not only not taken, but, instead, the phrase "community policing" was also distorted beyond recognition to mean almost the exact opposite to what the Bloomington School recommended. As Vincent Ostrom (1991b, 1997) would increasingly complain over the course of his life, the Orwellian distortion of language is a significant, understudied phenomenon in public choice.

## THE IMPOSSIBILITY OF EFFICIENT HIERARCHICAL PUBLIC ECONOMIES

The most important point made by V. Ostrom, Tiebout, and Warren (1961) is that, by analyzing the nature of public services that a metropolitan public administration has to solve, we are led to the conclusion that a consolidated, hierarchical administration would *unavoidably* lead to massive inefficiencies because *the administrative units operate at rigid scales, while the scale of public issues are varied and always changing.*

The idea behind this impossibility theorem is fairly simple: All complex societies face numerous collective issues, which, by their nature, occur at various scales, and, to make matters more complicated, these scales change all the time as a result of technology and other social processes. By contrast, the public administration units are relatively few in number (compared to the overall number of issues) and have relatively rigid geographical scales. As such, a given administrative unit is always faced with challenges that do not properly fit its administrative scale. This is true for administrative units at all scales. In a hierarchical system, when the scale of the problem is larger than the scale of administrative unit A, the responsibility for solving the problem goes to the larger administrative unit B, at a higher level. But B's scale can never fit exactly *all* the problems that are larger than A's scale. As such, the hierarchical system is bound to be rife with inefficiencies because A has only *one* higher level unit, B. To make matters worse, the logic of bureaucracy leads all administrative units to expand beyond their proper scope (Niskanen 1971).

By contrast, polycentric governance assumes that small-scale administrative units can organize on a quasi-ad hoc basis to address *some* of the larger scale problems (but not others). Different larger scale problems are addressed by different configurations of smaller scale units. We have seen this earlier. In their study of police departments across 80 metropolitan areas in the United States, Elinor Ostrom and her collaborators have found that police departments cooperated in precisely this diverse manner to take advantage of economies of scale with respect to criminal investigations, adult pretrial detention, and auxiliary services (such as crime labs and entry-level training) (E. Ostrom, Parks, and Whitaker 1978). As Ostrom, Tiebout, and Warren (1961) put it:

> [T]he statement that a government is "too large (or too small) to deal with a problem" often overlooks the possibility that the scale of the public and the political community need not coincide with that of the formal boundaries of a public organization. Informal arrangements between public organizations may create a political community large enough to deal with any particular public's problem. Similarly, a public organization may be able to constitute political communities within its boundaries to deal with problems that affect only a subset of the population. It would be a mistake to conclude that public organizations are of an inappropriate size until the informal mechanisms, which might permit larger or smaller political communities, are investigated.

These "informal mechanisms" are the alternative to the rigid hierarchical organization. We can also reframe the Ostrom–Tiebout–Warren impossibility theorem as an unavoidability theorem: Everywhere where politics works fairly well, that is, where the public sector is fairly responsive to citizens' needs and desires, we are bound to observe polycentric governance, rather than hierarchical governance. Vincent Ostrom stressed that the whole range of human affairs is polycentric (V. Ostrom 1991a, 224). Markets, science, common law, and competitive governance are standard examples of complex polycentric systems. But we also need to emphasize that this is just the beginning of the analysis. Not all polycentric systems are equally efficient. As we shall see in more detail in Chapter 4, Elinor Ostrom has shown that not all societies successfully self-govern, but only those that happen to zero-in on a number of so-called design principles.

Let us look more carefully at the reasons why, unlike polycentric governance, hierarchical public administration would be bound to be rife with inefficiencies.

## Control Over the Cause of the Problem

The cause of the problem must be under the control of the administrative unit. For example, a water pollution problem caused by a factory up the river, outside the jurisdiction of the local authority, cannot be solved by that local authority. This is often a real problem. In the 1960s, when Vincent Ostrom and his colleagues were writing, the following was happening:

> Pasadena, for example, is subject to severe smog attacks, but the city's boundary conditions do not cover an area sufficient to assure effective control of the appropriate meteorological and social space that would include the essential variables constituting a "smogisphere" of southern California. None of the separate cities of southern California, in fact, can encompass the problem. Instead, county air pollution control districts were organized for the Los Angeles metropolitan community. The failure of even those counties to meet adequately the criterion of effective control has led the Californian state government to assume an increasingly important role in smog control. (V. Ostrom, Tiebout, and Warren 1961)

The same holds for positive externalities. If an administrative unit is providing a public good it has to have a way of preventing free-riding. For instance, if one group acts responsibly in order to avoid overfishing, the problem is solved only if other groups are also prevented from overfishing. Mirroring what Buchanan and Tullock (1962, chaps. 5–6) would famously write a year later in *The Calculus of Consent*, they summarize: "A function of government, then, is to internalize the externalities—positive and negative—for those goods which the producers and consumers are unable or unwilling to internalize for themselves" (V. Ostrom, Tiebout, and Warren 1961).

This idea is far more general than just the concern with metropolitan governance. For example, in her studies of the common-pool resources management problems, Elinor Ostrom encountered again and again the importance of polycentricity, and she is

> urging readers to think more positively about complex, polycentric systems of governance that are created by individuals who have considerable autonomy to engage in self-governance. *Given the wide variety of ecological problems that individuals face at different scales, an important design principle is getting the boundaries of any one system roughly fit the ecological boundaries of the problem it is designed to address.* Since most ecological problems are nested from very small local ecologies to those of global proportions, following this principle requires substantial investment in governance systems at multiple levels—each with some autonomy but each exposed to information, sanctioning, and actions from below and above. (Elinor Ostrom 2005a, 258)

Notice the similarity to the challenges to metropolitan governance. And as there, we encounter the same intellectual difficulty here: "one of the important threats is the effort to impose uniform rules and large boundaries on systems so they are more comprehensible to academics

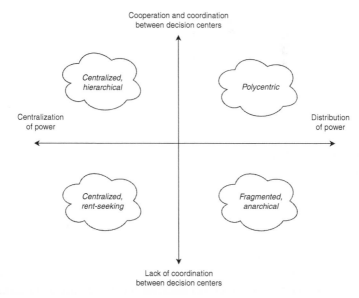

Figure 1.3.   **The Distinction between Polycentricity and Fragmentation.**

and policymakers" (Elinor Ostrom 2005a, 257). Also notice, that polycentricity is quite different from simply decentralization. Large-scale problems require large-scale solutions. The point isn't to *reduce* the scale of all administrative units, but to *fit* the scale of the administrative unit to the scale of the issue. This being said, the confusion between polycentricity and decentralization is somewhat understandable considering the fact that, in our world, overcentralization is far more common than undercentralization. As such, in practice, the concern for fitting the administrative unit to the scale of the problem often amounts to calling for decentralization—as we have seen in the example of policing.

One simple way to understand the difference between polycentricity and mere decentralization (and thus fragmentation) is to think in terms of the distinction proposed by Pahl-Wostl and Knieper and illustrated in Figure 1.3.

## Accurately Measuring the Demand for Public Goods and the Opportunity Cost of Providing Them

When the government is trying to fix a problem, the cost of the problem must be properly evaluated, for otherwise the administration might spend either too many or too few resources for tackling it. But public goods are notoriously difficult to evaluate because everyone is expecting others to shoulder the costs. For example, surveys are a somewhat imperfect method of assessing cost because people might complain about everything, far beyond the resources they are willing to contribute to address the problems. To put it differently, when somebody else is supposed to fix the problem, it's their job to find the resources to do it; our job is just to complain.

There is a more fundamental reason why the true demand for public goods is inherently difficult to evaluate:

> A decision to buy a particular good or service reflects willingness to forgo all other opportunities for which the money could have been used. An expression of demand in a market system always includes reference to what is forgone as well as what is purchased.
>
>     The articulation of preferences in the public sector often fails to take account of forgone opportunities.... Because most public goods and services are financed through a process of taxation involving no choice,

optimal levels of expenditure are difficult to establish. (V. Ostrom and Ostrom 1977, 185)

V. Ostrom, Tiebout, and Warren (1961) refer to this issue as the problem of "packageability," and note that "private goods, because they are easily packageable, are readily subject to measurement and quantification. Public goods, by contrast, are generally not so measurable." What they mean by this is that with private goods each person gets his or her own separate, individual good, while with public goods everyone gets the same shared good. This may make coercion necessary, in order to prevent free-riding, but

[w]hereas the income received for providing a private good conveys information about the demand for that good, payment of taxes under threat of coercion indicated only that taxpayers prefer paying taxes to going to jail. Little or no information is revealed about user preferences for goods procured with tax-supported expenditures. (V. Ostrom and Ostrom 1977, 175)

What this means is that "alternative mechanisms to prices are needed for articulating and aggregating demands into collective choices that reflect individuals' preferences for a particular quantity and/or quality of public goods or services" (V. Ostrom and Ostrom 1977, 175). But all such alternative mechanisms suffer from very serious problems. E. Ostrom and Whitaker (1973, chap. 8 in McGinnis 1999b, 179) noted this problem with respect to rigorously evaluating the outputs of police departments: "Police departments characteristically provide all services without consumer charges, even though some similar services are provided privately. Thus, the market value of police output cannot be obtained."

To make matters worse, a standard result in public choice is that a person's decisions as part of a collective, for example, when they vote, are far less careful than their personal decisions, because one has less control over the outcome (Buchanan 1954; Olson 1965, 1982, chap. 2; Caplan 2008). For instance, regardless of the candidate to whom you personally vote, the same candidate will win the election, so there's no point to regret your decision too much afterward. By contrast, if one buys the "wrong" car, one doesn't just have to live with it, but one can also justifiably regret not having made a different decision. This leads

to troubling conclusions with respect to how much attention people pay
to costs of publicly provided goods.

## Fiscal Equivalence and Redistribution

Mirroring Buchanan and Wagner's concerns in *Democracy in Deficit*
(1977), Vincent and Elinor Ostrom note that

> [c]osts must be proportioned to benefits if people are to have any sense of
> economic reality. Otherwise beneficiaries may assume that public goods
> are free goods, that money in the public treasury is "the government's
> money," and that no opportunities are forgone in spending that money.
> When this happens, the foundations of a democratic society are threat-
> ened. (V. Ostrom and Ostrom 1977, 186–87)

This problem of populist politicians promising "free goods" is of
course perpetually occurring, and the voting public is more or less
willing to let itself swayed by this illusion. Vincent and Elinor
Ostrom's note that an imperfect solution to this potentially large
problem is the idea of "fiscal equivalence" (Olson 1969). In *The
Calculus of Consent* in the chapter on the problem of pressure groups,
Buchanan and Tullock describe this possible solution as "requir[ing]
that individuals and groups securing differential benefits also bear
the differential costs" (Buchanan and Tullock 1962, 291). As we
shall see in Chapter 4, this concept of fiscal equivalence is one of the
major "design principles" for a sustainable social system, namely the
"Fairness principle: Proportionality between the benefits and costs of
various actors."

A problem with fiscal equivalence, as both Buchanan and Tullock
and Vincent and Elinor Ostrom recognized, is that it cannot deal very
well with "cases where over-all redistribution cannot be put aside"
(Buchanan and Tullock 1962, 292). Consider the following example:

> [S]uppose that the issue confronted is that of providing federal funds to
> aid the depressed coal-mining area of West Virginia. For such a measure
> the levy of special taxes on citizens of West Virginia would be self-
> defeating. Nevertheless, it is relatively easy to see that, if such aid is to
> be financed out of general tax revenue, a veritable Pandora's box may
> be opened. Depressed fishing villages along the Gulf coast, depressed
> textiles towns in New England, depressed automobile production

centers in Michigan, depressed zinc-mining areas in Colorado, etc., may all demand and receive federal assistance. As a result excessive costs will be imposed on the whole population. (Buchanan and Tullock 1962, 292–93)

The question is thus, how can we organize the system such that "[g]enuinely depressed areas, considered as such by the whole population, would tend to be provided with assistance without at the same time opening up the whole set of grants to areas not considered to be deserving of assistance" (Buchanan and Tullock 1962)? We can think of two possible solutions to this problem.

The first solution is to draw a lesson from how insurance companies deal with moral hazard. For example, in order to avoid people indulging in too many unnecessary and expensive medical procedures, insurance companies require copayment. By requiring patients to pay a fraction of the cost themselves, insurance companies try to introduce considerations of cost in the patients' decision as to whether to have a particular procedure. The same type of approach can be used to address the above problem, with the federal level requiring a certain level of copayment from the local level.

For example, this is how the European Union's structural funds work. In order to access these funds, usually provided to poorer members of the union by the richer members for specific projects, the recipient is required to cosponsor the project. You can understand this as implicitly forcing the recipients to rank the importance of various possible projects and ask for structural funds help only for the most important. Some of the more effective Eastern European governments, such as Poland, have managed to organize in this fashion relatively well, which has led to a high "absorption rate" of these funds (of the total funds available in principle, recipient countries usually manage to receive only a fraction because they cannot organize to provide the copayment). They have used such help to fund relatively important goods, such as building roads. Other, less-effective Eastern European governments, such as Romania, have been far less successful in absorbing the structural funds, which can be understood as a failure to organize collectively to rank the importance of various possible projects and cosponsor only the most important ones.

On the same grounds, Elinor Ostrom was critical of interventions in developing countries which did not take into account how the

intervention ends up distorting the recipients' incentives in perverse
ways, what is known as the Samaritan's Dilemma (Buchanan 1975;
Gibson et al. 2005):

> Showering a region with funds is a poor investment if that serves
> mainly to bolster political careers and builds little at the ground level.
> It makes more sense to invest modest levels of donor funds in local
> projects in which the recipients are willing to invest some of their own
> resources. If the level of external funding becomes very large without
> being strongly tied to a responsibility for repayment over time, local
> efforts at participation may be directed more at rent seeking than
> at productive investment activities. (Elinor Ostrom, interviewed by
> Aligica 2003)

Another possible solution stems from the analysis of the problem in
terms of "concentrated benefits and dispersed costs." Buchanan and
Tullock's "Pandora's box" is opened because each special interest
gets its concentrated benefit, while everyone gets stuck with the dispersed cost. For each case, the dispersed cost upon one individual is
very small, but it adds up. Paradoxically, everyone can end up worst
off because the amount they end up paying in total, a little bit by
a little bit, is lower then what they receive. Buchanan and Tullock
thought that one possible institutional solution to this problem would
be to organize the aid relationship on an equal size criterion: in order
to assure that the recipients and the providers have equal bargaining
power, they should be roughly the same in size. "For example, if the
designed aid to West Virginia were to be collected from special taxes
levied on Oklahoma only, then we could be assured that roughly
balancing political forces would determine the final outcome"
(Buchanan and Tullock 1962, 293). This sounds unusual, and, indeed,
it does not reflect the hierarchical approach currently in use. It would
describe instead a polycentric mutual aid system, in which providing assistance is paired with effective monitoring and assessment
of genuine need. The civil society mutual aid societies that existed
prior to the rise of the welfare state had precisely such a polycentric
organization, but this civil society system was largely replaced by
the rise of the welfare state (Beito 2000). To some extent, such civil
society organizations still exist in the realm of faith-based initiatives
(McGinnis 2008, 2010).

## The Separation of Production and Provision

One of the recurring themes in the Bloomington School is the fact that public services and goods that are "consumed collectively" can be produced by a variety of methods. Unlike the simplified perspective in most accounts of public economics, according to which public services are assumed almost by definition to be produced by a government agency, the Ostroms and their collaborators documented many hybrid institutions that do not fit well in either purely "state" or purely "market" categories. In contrast to this conflation between the public sphere and government,

> the work done at the Workshop demonstrates that public services need not be provided by a central government or the state. Many streets, roads, and other thoroughfares, fire protection, police services, and other such services may be arranged by local communities. These arrangements may rely on private entrepreneurs, but under terms and conditions that are communally specified.
>
> We need not think of "government" or "governance" as something provided by states alone. Families, voluntary associations, villages, and other forms of human association all involve some form of self-government. Rather than looking only to states, we need to give much more attention to building the kinds of basic institutional structures that enable people to find ways of relating constructively to one another and of resolving problems in their daily lives. (Vincent Ostrom, interviewed by Aligica 2003)

One way to make sense of hybrid public–private arrangements is to think about the distinction between *provision* (paying for the good) and *production* (creating the good). As noted by Oakerson and Parks (2011), "[o]ne key insight of V. Ostrom, Tiebout, and Warren (1961) almost forty years ago was that public provision did not require public production by the same governmental unit. Indeed, all governments provide services to their citizenry that they do not produce in-house." Oakerson and Parks (2011) also develop a more complex analysis of "provision." They note that, beyond just the decision to subsidize the production of a particular good, provision may also include public decisions about "what quantities of each service to provide and what quality standards to apply, and how to arrange for and monitor production" (Oakerson and Parks 2011). Such decisions about whether "to contract out and what to produce in-house is a city-specific decision," which "requires careful attention to the nature of specific public goods and services and the local market for their procurement" (Oakerson and Parks 2011). The institutional complexity of hybrid systems can be even greater. Elinor and Vincent Ostrom (1977) note that a government may obtain the desired public goods by a variety of methods such as

*Operating its own production unit.* E.g. a city with its own fire or police department.

*Contracting with a private firm.* E.g. a city that contracts with a private firm for snow removal, street repair, or traffic light maintenance.

*Establishing standards of service and leaving it up to each consumer to select a private vendor and to purchase service.* E.g. a city that licenses taxis to provide service, refuse collection firms to remove trash.

*Issuing vouchers to families and permitting them to purchase service from any authorized supplier.* E.g. a jurisdiction that issues food stamps, rent vouchers, or education vouchers, or operates a Medicaid program.

*Contracting with another government unit.* E.g. A city that purchases tax assessment and collection services from a county government unit, sewage treatment from a special sanitary district, and special vocational education services from a school board in an adjacent city.

*Producing some services with its own unit, and purchasing other services from other jurisdictions and from private firms.* E.g. a city with its own police patrol force, which purchases laboratory services from the county sheriff, joins with several adjacent communities to pay for a joint dispatching service, and pays a private ambulance firm to provide emergency medical transportation.

These kinds of arrangements, which are all quite common, allow a much more flexible public sector, but they do not fit very well in simple economic categories assuming clear distinctions between private and public, markets, and governments. They lead to what Richard Wagner (2014) has called "entangled political economy."

## NOTES

1. Stigler developed the theory of "regulatory capture" —the idea that existing firms influence the regulatory process and obtain regulations that harm their competitors. This is what explains why existing firms often support government regulations of their industries.

2. Olson (1965, 1982) developed and elaborated the consequences of the theory of "dispersed costs and concentrated benefits"—the idea that because the costs of laws that grant special privileges to specific groups are spread out over a large number of people, each suffering only a minor harm, those harmed are not going to bother to organize to counteract the legislation; by contrast, those receiving the privilege do organize because each of them is individually receiving a large benefit.

3. Niskanen (1971) developed the public choice theory of bureaucracy explaining why bureaucracies have unavoidable inefficiencies, no matter how well we may try to organize them.

4. Building on Tiebout (1956), Oates (1972, 1999) developed the theory of fiscal federalism, which tries to identify the efficient allocation of benefits and tax burdens at different levels.

# Chapter Two

# Polycentricity

## *The Art and Science of Association*

The most important lesson for public policy analysis derived from [my] intellectual journey ... is that humans have a more complex motivational structure and more capability to solve social dilemmas than posited in earlier rational-choice theory. Designing institutions to force (or nudge) entirely self-interested individuals to achieve better outcomes has been the major goal posited by policy analysts for governments to accomplish for much of the past half century.

Extensive empirical research leads me to argue that instead, a core goal of public policy should be to facilitate the development of institutions that bring out the best in humans. We need to ask how diverse polycentric institutions help or hinder the innovativeness, learning, adapting, trustworthiness, levels of cooperation of participants, and the achievement of more effective, equitable, and sustainable outcomes at multiple scales.

To explain the world of interactions and outcomes occurring at multiple levels, we also have to be willing to deal with complexity instead of rejecting it. ... When the world we are trying to explain and improve ... is not well described by a simple model, we must continue to improve our frameworks and theories so as to be able to understand complexity and not simply reject it. (Elinor Ostrom 2010a)

The great nineteenth-century French economist, Frédéric Bastiat, raised the following famous puzzle:

On coming to Paris for a visit, I said to myself: Here are a million human beings who would all die in a few days if supplies of all sorts did not flow into this great metropolis. It staggers the imagination to try to comprehend

Photo 3.  *Collective Photo at the First Edition of the Workshop on the Workshop (WOW1) Conference. (Source: The Workshop in Political Theory and Policy Analysis at Indiana University, 1977)*

the vast multiplicity of objects that must pass through its gates tomorrow, if its inhabitants are to be preserved from the horrors of famine, insurrection, and pillage. And yet all are sleeping peacefully at this moment, without being disturbed for a single instant by the idea of so frightful a prospect. On the other hand, eighty departments have worked today, without co-operative planning or mutual arrangements, to keep Paris supplied. How does each succeeding day manage to bring to this gigantic market just what is necessary—neither too much nor too little? What, then, is the resourceful and secret power that governs the amazing regularity of such complicated movements, a regularity in which everyone has such implicit faith, although his prosperity and his very life depend upon it? (Bastiat 1845, chap. 18)

One of the most basic, and arguably the most important, accomplishments of economics is to have solved this puzzle. No one is in charge of this gigantic decentralized process that brings supply roughly in equilibrium with demand across all markets at all times. And yet it happens. The reason why it happens is that prices provide the relevant information to both entrepreneurs and consumers about how to adjust their behaviors (Hayek 1945). When various entrepreneurs notice that the price of some goods or services is high relative to the cost of supplying them, they crowd-in to supply them. You can think of such entrepreneurs as acting purely out of self-interest, trying to earn the high possible profits before the competition gets too tough and pushes prices near the costs of supplying the goods or services. But their self-interested actions have socially beneficial effects, leading to consumers getting what they want. Paris gets fed. New things get invented. The costs of production go down and the luxuries of the past become the necessities of the present. On the other hand, when consumers see the price of X becoming high relative to the prices of some of its (imperfect) substitutes, they economize on X: they buy less of it or only buy it if they really need it. In other words, high prices send signals not only to entrepreneurs, but also to consumers. Both these processes work in the same direction and lead to the seamless adjustment of supply and demand. They lead to *widespread coordination among strangers*. They lead to coordination within a city like Paris, and to coordination in markets spanning the entire globe. They lead to coordination of short-term plans, as well as to long-term investment plans.

For the past two and a half centuries since the publication of Adam Smith's *Wealth of Nations*, understanding this process in which large-scale coordination is created "as if by an invisible hand" has blown the minds of every budding economist. And most professional economists seldom venture too far from this marvel. But notice *how* the marvel occurs. It only works because *prices* act as the coordination device that sends the signals.[1] However, there are many other aspects of our societies which do not involve prices, but, which, still require coordination. How does coordination happen outside the price system? The temptation is to assume that the *only* alternative to market coordination is hierarchical top-down control. This was indeed one of the common assumptions of transaction cost economics from Ronald Coase (1937) to Oliver Williamson (1992). The Bloomington School's concept of polycentricity is a direct challenge to this assumption. (V. Ostrom 1972, 1991a, Elinor Ostrom 1999, 2005a, chap. 9; McGinnis 1999b; Wagner 2005; McGinnis and Walker 2010; Aligica and Tarko 2012; Cole and McGinnis 2014; Boettke and Candela 2015).

We have already seen a flavor of this in the previous chapter. The different units, operating at different scales, which combine to produce police services in a metropolitan area, are not part of a single hierarchical system. Nonetheless, contrary to the expectations of many "experts" in the 1950s and 1960s, chaos did not reign. Coordination did happen. Economies of scales did get utilized.

Vincent Ostrom first developed the concept of polycentricity by generalizing into the realm of public economics the concept of markets, while at the same time avoiding the unrealistic perfect competition assumption of Tiebout's (1956) first model of institutional competition.[2] As we have seen, when the mainstream of the public administration profession was arguing in favor of consolidating the metropolitan administrations, the Ostroms dissented from this intuition. They developed a competing intuition thanks to an analogy to markets, which highlighted the potential efficiency of local public economies:

> Duplication of functions is assumed to be wasteful and inefficient. Presumably efficiency can be increased by eliminating "duplication of services" and "overlapping jurisdictions." Yet we know that efficiency can be realized in a market economy only if multiple firms serve the same market. Overlapping service areas and duplicate facilities are necessary conditions for the maintenance of competition in a market economy. Can we expect similar forces to operate in a public economy? (V. Ostrom and Ostrom 1977)

From their perspective, the most likely path to efficient public administration was not consolidation, but developing smart overarching rules that would allow productive "interorganizational arrangements." Such arrangements

> would manifest market-like characteristics and display both efficiency-inducing and error-correcting behavior. Coordination in the public sector need not, in those circumstances, rely exclusively upon bureaucratic command structures controlled by chief executives. Instead, the structure of interorganizational arrangements may create important economic opportunities and evoke self-regulating tendencies. (V. Ostrom and Ostrom 1977)

Half a century later, we have the empirical evidence regarding the validity of the polycentric perspective with respect to local public economies and with common-pool resources management. But such examples may still seem relatively simple. Perhaps the system of police services in a metropolitan area is not large enough to create serious impediments to the creation of informal interorganizational arrangements.

In his overview of different types of polycentric systems, Vincent Ostrom (1991a) lays out several much more challenging examples apart from markets and local public economies. They all have the same feature: they are (1) decentralized systems in which coordination happens without hierarchical command and control, and (2) they lack market prices for a coordination mechanism. How does coordination happen then? These are the hard cases of emergent social orders, and the concept of polycentricity aims to provide a framework for analyzing under what conditions we can expect such emergent orders to coordinate in a productive fashion. As Vincent Ostrom (1991a, 228) put it, "[t]he challenge is to understand how patterns of polycentricity might extend to the whole system of human affairs." Here are Vincent Ostrom's examples of polycentric systems: "(1) competitive market economies, (2) competitive public economies, (3) scientific inquiry, (4) law and adjudicatory arrangements, (5) systems of governance with a separation of powers and checks and balances, and (6) patterns of international order" (V. Ostrom 1991a, 228). Ostrom (1972) also discusses democratic politics as "polycentricity in the selection of political leadership and the organization of political coalitions."

Before looking more carefully at the theory, let us explore some of these examples in a bit more detail. And while exploring such examples, bear in mind that what is at stake in the attempt to build a theory of polycentricity is "nothing less than a theory of hidden order, a theory of an 'invisible hand' directing the 'social mechanism.' If articulated, such a theory might be applicable to many instances of social order, in different arenas and at different social levels" (Aligica 2013, 47). Or, as Vincent Ostrom (1972) put it, "[p]enetrating an illusion of chaos and discerning regularities that appear to be created by an 'invisible hand' imply that the tasks of scholarship... will be presented with serious difficulties.... Patterns and regularities which occur under an illusion of chaos may involve an order of complexity that is counterintuitive."

It is also interesting to point out that the *Public Choice* journal and the early members of what became the Public Choice Society, before settling on the name "public choice," had gathered their research agenda under the title "Papers on non-market decision making." We can see polycentricity as a key element of this agenda.

Beyond the purely scientific interest in building such a theory of productive emergent orders, more general than just the theory of markets, having an understanding of the conditions under which we can depart from hierarchical organizations without descending into chaos is crucially important for building viable democratic societies in which citizens have as much control as possible over the rules to which they are subjected. In *Understanding Institutional Diversity*, Elinor Ostrom starts her account of polycentricity with this concern:

[O]fficials and policy analysts who presume that they have the right design can be dangerous. They are likely to assume that citizens are short-sighted and motivated only by extrinsic benefits and costs. Somehow, the officials and policy analysts assume that they have different motivations and can find optimal policy because they are not directly involved in the problem …. They are indeed isolated from the problems. This leaves them with little capability to adapt and learn in light of information about outcomes resulting from their policies. All too often, these "optimal" policies have Leviathan-like characteristics to them. (Elinor Ostrom 2005a, 256)

By contrast, "polycentric systems are … complex, adaptive systems without one central authority dominating all of the others" (Elinor Ostrom 2005a, 284). And, by providing an overarching conceptual umbrella, the theory of polycentricity may help us draw analogies from the study of type of system upon another:

[P]olycentricity … provides a unified conceptual framework for analyzing and comparing … different forms of social self-organization as special cases of a more general unique evolutionary phenomenon. This phenomenon is manifesting in social groups and networks made up of very different kinds of actors (from scientists to entrepreneurs to politicians to judges to urban planners to military leaders) and relative to very different kinds of overarching end goals (such as truth seeking, maximizing economic profits, gaining and maintaining political power, seeking justice, or maintaining social order). Understanding these social phenomena as special cases of polycentricity may make it easier to draw informed analogies from one field to another. (Aligica and Tarko 2012)

## A FEW EXAMPLES OF LARGE-SCALE POLYCENTRIC SYSTEMS

### The Scientific Community

The concept of "polycentricity" was first introduced by British polymath Michael Polanyi (1951), for the purpose of analyzing the decentralized structure of the scientific community (Polanyi 1962; Aligica and Tarko 2012; Tarko 2015a)[3]. Although this may sound farfetched now, in the 1950s a large number of people, including many scientists themselves, were seriously arguing for the complete centralization and "rationalization" of the organization of the scientific community. These calls were very similar in nature to the calls to centralize the public administration in urban areas, the main argument resting on the claim that the duplication of efforts was wasteful. Hierarchical organization was supposed to eliminate this waste. Scientists would no longer waste resources studying the same things in parallel, and competing with each other, but they would instead cooperate to the benefit of all. But, as Polanyi argued, a hierarchical organization would also severely diminish freedom of inquiry and ultimately destroy science. Given that the aim of science is *discovery*, pushing our knowledge further than it is now, the best avenues for research cannot possibly be known beforehand. This may be obvious to you, but that's because you have grown in a very different intellectual climate than the British intellectuals of the first half of the twentieth century, who were mostly Fabian socialists (White 2012, chap. 7).

The scientific community is a very large-scale, decentralized, international organization lacking any central management or a formalized legislative or rule-enforcement body. Even the entry/exclusion rules are lax and unclear. By many standards it should not work. But instead it is one of the most successful human endeavors of all time.

Even if we partition the scientific community by discipline, these communities are still very large. For example, the economics community currently has almost 34,000 registered members at IDEAS Research Papers in Economics, and there are currently over 200,000 registered authors at the Social Science Research Network. The American Chemical Society has over 164,000 members, working both in the academia and in the private sector (almost 25,000 of them are professors). According to the American Institute of Physics, only in United States there are over 10,000 physics and astronomers working in the academia. The Society of Biology has about 80,000 members.

Interestingly for such a large community, the norms and rules of the scientific community are mostly cultural and informal. They have no constitution laying down the rules, for example, of how peer review should be made or about the "scientific method" that should be used, and no monopolistic governing body enforcing such rules and deciding who is or isn't part of the scientific community. It has no geographic barriers, and yet it manages to delineate membership in a decentralized and largely informal manner (single organizations and associations may have formalized internal rules, but not the community as a whole). Experiments with new rules, such as open-access publishing and preprints archives without peer review, and new associations created without a need for permission from higher bodies, are a natural and significant part of the system.

It is commonly claimed that communities larger than about a hundred people cannot possibly work effectively without formal rules and some form of central management and monopoly enforcement of those rules. For example, Dixit (2003) claims that "[h]onesty is self-enforcing only between pairs of sufficiently close neighbors. Global honesty prevails only in a sufficiently small world. The extent of self-enforcing honesty is likely to decrease when the world expands beyond this size." These claims are a result of a theoretical model. But if Dixit's model would have been empirically valid, and not merely internally consistent, it would be a demonstration that science was literally impossible.

The scientific community highlights the fact that polycentric governance can and do, at least sometimes, scale up, even in the absence of formalized and centralized control. As Polanyi (1951, 1962) originally has argued, science is so successful precisely *because* of its decentralized and quasi-anarchic organization. The polycentric nature of the scientific community is evident even within a specific domain. There are multiple research centers each with its own somewhat different research agenda and preferred methods of investigation. Journals and publishing houses also often lean in one direction or another either explicitly (in their stated mission) or informally (due to the personal idiosyncrasies of their editors).

Science is thus essentially anarchic in the sense that there are no official leaders, no universal research method, and the entire process works on the basis of a complex and ever-changing *prestige network*. The impact of scientific publications, that is, their popularity and usefulness within the scientific community, and implicitly the impact of the journals and publishing houses that publish them and of the academic institutions that create the research, is what generates the evolution in time of this prestige network. *It is this prestige network that provides the mechanism for large-scale coordination*, the mechanism that works in a roughly similar way to which prices work to coordinate markets. And the norms of science, although informal, operate as the overarching system of rules which makes the entire enterprise possible:

> The "sovereign will," in this case, is the concurrence of others in the scientific community rather than some ultimate authority who exercises monopoly control over rulership prerogatives and instruments of coercion. Polanyi explicitly recognizes that a polycentric order among scientific investigators entails normative presuppositions that respect the search for truth, desire justice, and maintain mutual respect and reciprocity in their relationships with one another. ... Science as a polycentric order depends, then, upon an autonomous pursuit of inquiry that requires a reciprocal respect for the autonomy of others. Contestability in the realm of ideas is an essential feature of science as such an order. Tensions must necessarily exist in such circumstances, but the reward for participating in contestable arguments in respectful ways is to reap the fruit of tilling the field of knowledge as civilization advances. (V. Ostrom 1991a, 233–34)

## Common Law

Another interesting case of a large-scale polycentric system is the system of law and adjudicatory arrangements. Vincent Ostrom (1991a, 236) notes that, historically, "[t]he achievement of polycentricity in the function of the judiciary and the maintenance of a rule of law was an important step in the development of Western civilization." This is a difficult process for the following reasons:

> The possibility of conceptualizing courts and the judicial process as a polycentric order will depend upon the development of (1) legal concepts and terms that can be known in a public interpersonal context, (2) legal criteria that can be used as a basis for judgment, and (3) methods of legal reasoning that can be used to organize thoughts and array evidence for the same purpose. Unless a community of agreement (in other words, substantial consensus) can exist regarding legal concepts, criteria for choice or judgment, and methods of legal reasoning, there can be no basis for a polycentric ordering. (V. Ostrom 1991a, 235)

The challenge of a customary or common law system is to generate a "rule of law"; in other words, to generate coordination among independent judges with respect to what is allowed and what isn't allowed, and also with respect to the penalties for different offenses (Hayek

1973; Hasnas 2005). At the risk of oversimplifying, we can understand how this coordination occurs in the following way.

At its origin, in the eleventh to twelfth century, the common law system comprised many competing legal subsystems. Legal providers were not clients of the same political patron. The king and the church politically challenged each other, and collected their rents from their own courts. The environment created by this rivalry permitted systems with no organized patron to survive, such as Equity Courts, Staple Courts, or Law Merchant. This additional competition further constrained all participants. Today, the competition between legal systems persists, on one hand, thanks to private adjudication (Stringham 2015), and, on the other hand, thanks to variations between jurisdictions.

This competitiveness made judges quite sensitive to matters of reputation. If their decisions ended up routinely discarded in future cases, their reputation would go down and fewer people would be willing to use their courts. This concern led them to lay out in detail the justification for their decision, which in turn can serve to inform decisions in future cases. We can thus see the reliance on precedent as emerging within customary law, rather than being there from the beginning by design (Hasnas 2005).

The customary/common law system is thus a polycentric system in which judges are formally independent, but in practice operate under the constraint of legal precedents. In such a system, the rule of law is an emergent feature. This is different from the Napoleonic civil law system in which legislatures have the task to write down the laws, and courts only decide whether the law was broken. The current rough consensus within the empirical law and economics literature is that the common law system is somewhat more efficient than the civil law system (see Rubin 1977; Mahoney 2001; La Porta, Lopez-de-Silanes, and Shleifer 2008), although authors like John Hasnas argue that the current American system has virtually morphed into the Napoleonic system.

## Federalism

The theory of federalism developed by Vincent Ostrom and the Bloomington School has a distinct peculiarity due to the fact that federalism is understood as a type of polycentricity (Bish 1999). Conversely, Elinor Ostrom's account of polycentricity (Elinor Ostrom 2005a, chap. 9) draws inspiration from Vincent's account of federalism

(V. Ostrom 1987, 1991b). As such, while "economists generally consider federalism to consist of levels of government, each with clearly defined and nonoverlapping jurisdiction over particular functions," Vincent Ostrom strongly dissented, arguing instead that "[t]here is no hierarchy of governments" in the U.S. federal system (Bish 2014).

When Vincent Ostrom writes that the "principles of federalism permit people to function through self-governing institutions among local, regional, and national communities of interest in organizing collective endeavors" (V. Ostrom 1987, 173), he means that these different arenas are available simultaneously at all times—in other words, the jurisdictions are overlapping, rather than having carefully separated domains of responsibility.

Furthermore, the American federalism cannot be said to be hierarchical because the federal government cannot issue orders to local governments in the way in which, in a firm, a higher level manager can issue orders to a lower level employee. Conflicts are not only possible, but are also a common occurrence. For example, in recent years, various U.S. states have adopted drug laws, such as legalizing marijuana, that are clearly at odds with federal laws.

Perhaps the most eloquent presentation of just how different the Bloomington School account of federalism is can be found in Elinor Ostrom's article "Size and performance in a federal system" (1976, chap. 10 in McGinnis 1999b). In this article, she reframes the analysis of police studies, described in the previous chapter, as an application in the theory of federalism. This article, published in *Publius*, the main journal of studies of federalism, is bound to look strange when we compare it to other accounts, such as Weingast (1995). What makes it unusual is that the focus of attention is not on relationships between "levels of government," but on *individual citizens* who live their lives embedded in a federal structure, and having access to various public and private agencies at the same time. The focus is on whether the institutional structure does a good job at satisfying individual concerns.

From this point of view, federalism is an institutional arrangement by means of which the organization of public administration tries to take into account the subjectivity and diversity of people's preferences. Different people demand different kinds of public goods and have different aspiration levels for the quality of each of them, and also have different views about what amounts to a reasonable cost. How do we build societies that allow as many people as possible to live their lives as they please? This problem of heterogeneity is undoubtedly one of the most fundamental challenges to building self-governing systems (Aligica and Tarko 2013; Aligica 2013).

Going back to the framework of *The Calculus of Consent*, the question is whether we can have a viable "invisible hand" mechanism operating in the political realm (and other social realms) in the same way as we have one in the market realm:

> Adam Smith and those associated with the movement he represented were partially successful in convincing the public at large that, within the limits of certain general rules of action, the self-seeking activities of the merchant and the moneylender tend to further the interests of everyone in the community. An acceptable theory of collective choice can perhaps do something similar in pointing the way toward *those rules for collective choice-making, the constitution, under which the activities of political tradesmen can be similarly reconciled with the interests of all members of the social group.* (Buchanan and Tullock 1962, 22, emphasis added)

The concept of polycentricity may provide precisely the insight to deal with such "political tradesmen," or, to use the Bloomington School preferred term, "public entrepreneurs" (Oakerson and Parks 1988; McGinnis 2016).

## POLYCENTRICITY AS A FRAMEWORK FOR THE ANALYSIS OF EMERGENT ORDERS

What do all such systems have in common? Polycentric systems are characterized by many autonomous decision centers which are formally independent but functionally interdependent. What we mean by "functionally interdependent" is simply that the decision centers create significant externalities upon each other, which makes it necessary for them to develop some overarching rules governing their interactions. First of all, these overarching rules can and often are created, monitored, and enforced by the decision centers themselves, rather than by an outside agency (e.g., a central government). Second, these overarching rules distinguish between legitimate and illegitimate activities of the decision centers, that is, which harms need to be compensated and which do not. Depending on the nature of these overarching rules, the polycentric system generates a more or less successful emergent order.

## Complex Adaptive Systems

There are no general principles for distinguishing "legitimate" from "illegitimate" activities. This distinction emerges endogenously from the interactions of the decision centers—it is the outcome of a multiparty Coasian bargain process in the presence of often large transaction costs. For instance, markets are an example of a polycentric system, with different competing firms and different consumers being the independent decision centers. An innovative firm disrupting the market and causing other firms to go bankrupt and many consumers to be unemployed is engaged in what's deemed a legitimate activity and does not need to compensate the harmed parties. By contrast, a firm massively polluting a river is deemed to be engaged in an illegitimate activity which requires compensation of the harmed parties. The overarching rules for markets, enabling them by delineating and enforcing property rights but also regulating them, allow for some of these harms to occur while eliminating others. This involves certain trade-offs: for example, preserving the benefits resulting from "permissionless innovation" at the expense of some occasional harms to various groups (Aligica and Tarko 2014a, chap. 4; Thierer 2016).

As we've seen in the previous chapter, the decision centers in local public economies can address a wide range of problems, and the solutions to each of these problems can have very different optimal scales (V. Ostrom, Tiebout, and Warren 1961). This means that decision centers have to find a way to face the problem that the scales of operation of administrative units are rigid, while problems are fluid and come at varied, and changing, scales. As Ostrom, Tiebout, and Warren (1961) first noted, and as Elinor Ostrom and her collaborators later documented across a wide range of examples, the solution to this administrative rigidity problem is to have smaller administrative units cooperate on a quasi-ad hoc basis to address larger scale problems as they appear. The side effect of this solution is that, rather than having a hierarchical public administration organization, we are left, by necessity, with a polycentric one.

This is also a complex, adaptive order. An order that is in constant flux, and which reacts to changing conditions. Different decision centers are constantly engaged in mutual adjustment, both in terms of competing with one another and in terms of cooperating to solve larger scale problems (McGinnis 2016). Furthermore, in line with their heterogeneity of beliefs and preferences, the cooperation is conditional, involving a certain degree of conflict, as well as entry and exit from larger associations.

As a result of this adaptive nature, polycentric systems don't have purely deliberate outcomes. Similar to a market, the outcome of the operation of a polycentric system is an emergent order which has certain unplanned features. We don't know for sure what science will discover tomorrow, or in what ways common law will change in a few decades from now, or which issues will become more or less centralized in a responsive self-governing federal system. These emergent features may be more or less desirable. And different people may disagree about this.

The way in which people in a polycentric system deal with undesirable outcomes is by trying to alter the set of overarching rules, such that the emergent outcome will be improved; for example, by limiting some negative externalities or by making broader use of the knowledge discovered by one decision center. Figure 2.1, adapted from the frameworks proposed by Aligica and Tarko (2012) and McGinnis (2016), tries to make sense of this adaptive process made possible by polycentricity. It includes: (1) the operational-level process, concerned with the actual production of public goods and the emergent system-level order; (2) the collective-choice process, concerned with identifying problems, giving voice to different points of view about each problem, and reforming the overarching set of rules.

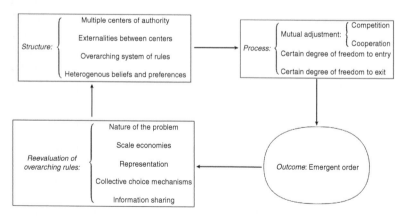

Figure 2.1. The Structure and Operation of a Polycentric System. Adapted from Aligica and Tarko and McGinnis (2016).

To summarize,

> Polycentricity emerges as a nonhierarchical institutional and cultural framework that makes possible the coexistence of multiple centers of decision-making with different objectives and values, and which sets the stage for an evolutionary competition between the complementary ideas and methods of these different decision centers. (Aligica 2013, 55)

We're going to return to this type of problem in Chapter 5, looking at the problem of complex adaptive systems from the related but somewhat different perspective of the Institutional Analysis and Development (IAD) framework. The IAD framework is much more focused on actually describing the rules which, ultimately, are responsible for generating the emergent outcomes.

## Vincent Ostrom's Polycentricity Conjecture

Let me end this chapter with what Paul Aligica and Michael McGinnis have occasionally referred to as one of the most intriguing and provocative ideas put forward by Vincent Ostrom. The validity of this idea is still quite uncertain. Unlike the Ostrom–Tiebout–Warren impossibility theorem, this one is more of an interesting conjecture. According to this conjecture, different polycentric systems, such as markets, democratic politics, federalism, common law, science, and peaceful international relations, rely upon each other and reinforce each other. If one or some of them are centralized and made less polycentric, the others are, in turn, also made more vulnerable. As Vincent Ostrom (1991a, 237) put it, "[p]olycentricity in each unit of government, then, is essential to the maintenance of polycentricity in 'the whole system of human affairs.'"

Or, as Aligica (2013, 50–51) put it:

> [O]ne of Ostrom's most interesting conjectures was that the structure and dynamics of a polycentric system is a function of polycentrism in the governance of adjoined systems. The basic social functions and institutional domains of a society can be organized in various degrees under a polycentric order: polycentricity in the structure of governmental arrangements, in economic affairs, in political processes, in judicial affairs, and in constitutional rule.

Polycentricity is a complex system of powers, incentives, rules, values, and individual attitudes, all combined in a complex system of relationships at different levels. One may detect very interesting dynamics at work. Market polycentrism seems to entail judicial polycentrism. Judicial polycentrism entails political polycentrism, and in its turn political polycentrism entails constitutional polycentrism. Accepting the existence of such a systemic logic, one may visualize the entire social system as defined by underlining currents originating in pulsating polycentric domains. Polycentric order in one area entails and produces polycentrism in other areas.

## NOTES

1. This also explains "market failures," which are situations in which the price of X doesn't fully reflect the opportunity cost of producing X, that is, the value of the other things that could have been produced if the resources wouldn't have been used for making X. For example, if there are third parties that are harmed but are not compensated, this harm is part of the opportunity costs of producing X, but it is not included in the price of X (which results from the market transactions). Hence, when such "spillover effects" are present, the price system leads to an imperfect form of coordination—the prices send "wrong" signals and resources can get misallocated or overused.

2. Bish (2014) argues that "Vincent's work is very similar to that of the Austrian economists, especially van Mises (1949) and Hayek (1945, 1960)" who "are not focused on equilibrium and optimization; they focus on information, incentives, innovation, adjustments, and feedback." Boettke, Lemke and Palagashvili (2014) elaborate a similar claim.

3. This section is adapted from Tarko (2015a).

# Chapter Three

# Escaping the Tragedy of the Commons

## The Concept of Property and the Varieties of Self-Governing Arrangements

In general, I am not opposed to modeling and using models for policy analysis. I am opposed to the persistent reliance upon models like "prisoners' dilemma" or the metaphor of "the tragedy of the commons," after years of empirical research in both the lab and the field has called their universal applicability into question. Many researchers drawing on these models have concluded that the participants in a commons dilemma are trapped in an inexorable process from which they cannot extract themselves. It is then inferred that external authorities are necessary to impose rules and regulations on local resource users who are otherwise incapable of saving themselves.... However, empirical research does not support the idea that a central agency could solve all resource problems for a large region with simple, top down directives. Field studies in all parts of the world have found that local groups of resource users, sometimes by themselves and sometimes with the assistance of external actors, have created a wide diversity of institutional arrangements for cooperating with common-pool resources. Field studies have also found multiple cases where resource users have failed to self-organize. (Elinor Ostrom, interviewed by Aligica 2003)

The life of a shepherd illustrates one of the simplest and most widely discussed social dilemmas: people pursuing their self-interest leading to negative social consequences. As a shepherd, you own a fairly large number of sheep and, to feed them, you take them up the mountain to one pasture or another. The sheep eat the grass, but the grass grows back, so there's no problem. Suppose, however, that you are not the only shepherd. Several others use the same pastures to feed their sheep.

Photo 4. *Elinor Ostrom with Members of the Irrigation Management Systems Study Group during Field Work in Nepal (The Workshop in Political Theory and Policy Analysis at Indiana University, 1994).*

If there are too many of you, bringing too many sheep up the mountain, the pastures can be severely damaged and everyone's interests will suffer. But here's the issue: If you unilaterally decide to keep fewer sheep, this doesn't solve the problem. You only hurt your own profits, without improving the situation all that much. And the same applies to everyone else. No one will reduce the size of their herd because you all need to do so. To put it differently, absent some mechanism for cooperation, you will all end up in a situation that all of you would like to avoid.

This problem, known as the *tragedy of the commons* (Hardin 1968), occurs again and again in numerous contexts. For example, overfishing problems are due to the exact same logic. Each fisherman faces the incentive to fish as much as he can because, if he doesn't, others will deplete the fish stock anyway. Or, consider flood protection. Building a dike is an expensive and time-consuming enterprise, but, if others in your area build the dike, they cannot help the fact that you are also going to benefit from the flood protection it provides. As a result, too many people may simply try to free-ride on others' efforts and not enough funds will be available to actually build an effective dike. Pollution problems are also similar. For instance, each car owner has the possibility to voluntarily install an emission filter, and if enough of them would do it, pollution would diminish. But why would anyone spend money for a filter, engaging in a costly purchase that might prove useless if many others don't do the same? Or why would any car company spend money on building a lower emission engine, increasing the cost of their cars, if the other car companies are not guaranteed to do the same?

There are other, more subtle examples, in which the common resource is not that obvious, but which suffer from the same structure of incentives. To fully appreciate the importance of the underlining logical structure of the tragedy of the commons, here are a few less-obvious examples.

In the early days of the London Stock Exchange, in the eighteenth century, investors faced a serious problem trying to differentiate trustworthy from untrustworthy traders:

> In the tragedy-of-the-commons story, when an area (such as a fishery or a pasture or in this case a stock market) has certain benefits, newcomers will not consider how their actions decrease the well-being of everyone else in that space. This was definitely a problem in the stock market. Although cheaters could make out like bandits, the more widespread cheating became, the more the market would shrivel. Even if interlopers know their actions will harm the market, they have little incentive to do otherwise.... With time bargainings that had settlements months in the future, one's counterpart might intentionally disappear or unintentionally become bankrupt in the interim. (Stringham 2015, 67–68)

Because, at the time, the government considered the stock market illegitimate, and actually actively tried to stop it, "brokers did not have the ability to rely on courts, so instead they figured out various ways to exclude defaulters" such as "writ[ing] the names of defaulters on a blackboard as a warning to others not to deal with them" (Stringham 2015, 68–69). As the stock market grew, these rules evolved, reaching the complex array of disclosure requirements that stock markets have today (Stringham 2015, chap. 6).

The same underlining structural problem also exists in the realm of politics. Why do special interests often succeed in getting favorable regulations even when those regulations hurt the majority? For example, since 1982, the restrictions on sugar imports have led to sugar being twice as expensive in the United States relative to international markets. This makes a wide variety of goods more expensive and also determines the attempts to substitute sugar with other products (e.g., corn syrup). The U.S. Congressional Budget Office estimated in 2015 that consumers in the United States spent 3.5 billion dollars more than they would have if the sugar import restriction was not in place (CfSR 2016). This is a huge sum of money that could have financed other economic activities. Why does such an inefficient policy exist? The answer is *concentrated benefits and dispersed costs* (Olson 1965). The cost to consumers is dispersed: about 10 dollars per person per year. Few people are going to bother to lobby the government to eliminate the sugar tariff for the sake of gaining $10 a year. As far as consumers are concerned, they are in a tragedy of the commons. By contrast, the beneficiaries of the policy, the domestic sugar producers, are relatively few in number and each gains tremendously from the sugar import restriction. Consequently, they are going to spend resources to lobby in favor of the policy.

Probably the most dramatic example of a tragedy of the commons is from the realm of farming. The so-called Great Leap Forward in China, between 1958 and 1961, amounted to a nationalization of individually owned farms, and the employment of farmers in large-scale state communal farms. This was supposed to generate significant increases in productivity due to presumed economies of scale. The effect of this policy was, instead, to create a tragedy of the commons on a massive scale. When farmer own their farms, having the right to keep what they produce, as well as the right to sell the excess production, gives them the incentive to produce as efficiently and as much as possible. By contrast, when the same farmers work on collectivized farms and each only gets a small share of the total production, all of them have the incentive to free-ride on other people's hard work— with the effect that no one is going to work very hard. As a result of this collectivization policy, agricultural production collapsed, and a massive famine followed. According to various estimates, between 20 and 43 million people starved to death (Peng 1987). In some areas, the death rate more than doubled compared to the previous years (Figure 3.1). Why did such a disaster occur? Before the "Great Leap Forward," the population was able to increase thanks to gradual increases of agricultural productivity, which created enough food to sustain the larger population. But then, with the abrupt change of

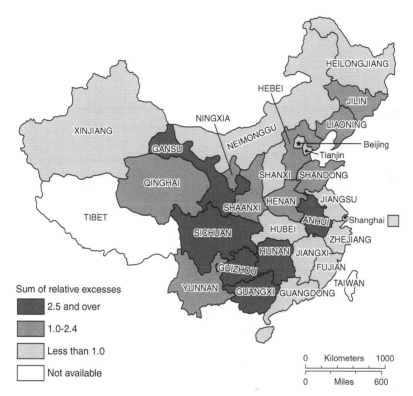

**Figure 3.1.** Increase in Mortality During the "Great Leap Forward" (1958–61), Relative to 1956–57. (Source of the image and data: Peng 1987.)

policy on a massive scale, the unexpected collapse of agricultural productivity left tens of millions suddenly without food.

One of the beauties of economic science, and game theory in particular, is that it helps us see that the *same* underlining structure is present behind such a wide variety of apparently very different social phenomena. As Elinor Ostrom remembered,

Game Theory has been very, very important in our work in that we've been able to take game-theoretic models and put them in the lab and test them. And thus my early exposure in the 1980s to the work of Reinhardt Selten, who is himself a Nobel Laureate, was a very, very important step in my training.... Classical Game Theory is very predictive in some environments but not fully predictive, by any manner/means, in an environment which is a social dilemma. But [it's] very helpful for us in analyzing and, as we develop a behavioral theory of humans and of other formal mechanisms, we can explain why people do cooperate in some settings and not others. (Smith 2009)

A social dilemma is a case in which individual rationality (everyone doing what's in their own personal interest) leads to unfortunate social consequences (Tullock 2005). The tragedy of the commons is the paradigmatic example of a social dilemma. People successfully cooperate in some contexts because they discover which specific rules can be put in place to solve the social dilemma, that is, to change the incentives faced by individuals such that their own personal interests become harmonized with broader social goals. In other cases, they may put in place rules that don't work that well or they may completely fail to reach any consensus about the rules, which explains the institutional failures we also see.

At the same time, this underlining similarity revealed by game theory can be deceptive. The fact that the same type of problem occurs in different contexts does *not* mean that the same solution will work everywhere. Why not? We need to bear in mind the distinction between *why* and *how*, that is, between the social function played by certain rules (*why* those rules are necessary) and the exact details of *how* to best fulfill this function in a given context. The presence of a common game theoretical structure behind many only tells us that the same "why" is at work across all these examples—but this does not tell us what *specific rules* need to be put in place from case to case. The warning against presumed "panaceas" or "one-size-fits-all" solutions was a recurrent leitmotif in Elinor Ostrom's work (E. Ostrom 2007; Elinor Ostrom, Janssen, and Anderies 2007; Elinor Ostrom and Cox 2010), precisely because many people neglect this distinction between why and how.

For example, when analyzing forests management, they discovered that forests are unexpectedly complex systems. Looking across numerous case studies they found such a variation of local institutions that it undermined "the view that template forest policies are likely to work when imposed on a country as a whole" (Gibson, McKean, and E. Ostrom 2000, 5).

These fieldwork case studies were done in Bolivia, Ecuador, India, Nepal, and Uganda as part of the International Forestry Resources and

Institutions research program (Gibson, McKean, and Ostrom 2000). Another example of the type of empirical work the Bloomington School has done are the extensive case studies of groundwater management in various parts of the United States. These were started by Vincent Ostrom. Elinor Ostrom's PhD dissertation was part of this larger project (E. Ostrom 1965). Later important studies were performed by Elinor Ostrom's doctoral students William Blomquist and Edella Schlager (e.g. see Blomquist, Schlager, and Heikkila 2004; Schlager and Blomquist 2008). They have also done extensive studies of irrigation systems around the world (Elinor Ostrom 1992).

Engaging in such empirical studies is necessary for getting a feel of the uncertainties and complexities involved, but their work also consisted in an effort to synthesize a very large preexisting literature. The extensive case studies literature of the management of common properly spanned thousands of examples. They formed a "vast amount of highly specialized knowledge ... without much synthesis or application of the knowledge to the policy problems involved" (Elinor Ostrom 1990, xv). This was partly due to the cross-disciplinary nature required by such a synthesis effort. The case studies came from "rural sociology, anthropology, history, economics, political science, forestry, irrigation sociology, and human ecology" and the authors of these studies "had cited primarily studies conducted by others in their own disciplines ... [f]ew citations had come from outside each author's disciplinary, sectoral, or regional frame of reference" (Elinor Ostrom 1990, xv). Moreover, the different studies were performed based on a wide variety of theoretical assumptions. Not all of them could be used for a proper *institutional* analysis focused on the "rules of the game" and the incentive structure created by these rules. Nonetheless, this huge literature complemented the empirical studies performed by the Bloomington School itself, and formed the basis for their stunning synthesizing effort. As Elinor Ostrom pointed out, "[s]ome years of hard work were required simply to read sufficient number of cases, study earlier efforts to synthesize findings from specialized fields, and develop coding forms" (Elinor Ostrom 1990, xvi).

We can see a clear similarity between this type of research and the earlier metropolitan debate. As before, the Bloomington School attacked the mainstream position in economics and political science for basically jumping to a set of conclusions that were empirically misinformed. As before, their attack came on two fronts: (1) marshalling an impressive amount of empirical evidence challenging what the mainstream mistakenly *imagined* to be the case, and (2) providing an alternative theoretical framework for making sense of the actual data. In the case of the metropolitan debate, the alternative theoretical framework (Vincent Ostrom's polycentricity idea) came before the empirical studies, and motivated their initial suspicions regarding the consolidationists' claims. In this case, they first faced the facts, and for a long time they were quite puzzled about how to make sense of them. What was wrong with the standard game theoretical account? It was not obvious. What was clear was that Hardin's theoretical approach to the tragedy of the commons and Olson's theory of collective action were deficient—they predicted that one could never observe what lots of researchers were in fact observing all over the world.

There were two important theoretical pieces that helped solve the puzzle. On one hand, they made use of the new theory of property rights developed by Harold Demsetz and Armen Alchian, which allows us to account for more complex property rights arrangements than just "private" versus "state." On the other hand, the penny finally dropped when, turning to game theory, Elinor Ostrom realized what the mistaken unstated assumption had been all along: mainstream theory assumed that people were *stuck* within a game, powerless to change it. The game payoffs were simply *given*. No attention was paid on how the players themselves might change the game.

## BEYOND MARKETS AND GOVERNMENTS

When Elinor Ostrom entered the debate about the tragedy of the commons, the standard view in the economics profession was that only two possibilities existed for trying to escape the tragedy (Hardin 1968): either privatization or centralized government control, when privatization was not feasible. Within public choice theory, a similar approach was gaining ground thanks to Mancur Olson's *Logic of Collective Action* (1965); Elinor Ostrom sometimes joked that it should've been called *The Logic of Collective Inaction* as it seemed to imply that only small groups could ever manage to effectively organize for collective action (as in the sugar tariff example above).

Both Vincent and Elinor Ostrom were taken aback by the popularity of Hardin's simplistic argument, as they had witnessed the contrary first hand in their earlier studies of water management and fisheries.

As discussed in the introduction, when Vincent Ostrom was hired as a consultant for the drafting of the Natural Resources article in the Alaskan Constitution, he was already fully familiar that complex collective action solutions are possible and that people often succeed in crafting them. Moreover, the Tocquevillian background to Bloomington School's approach to political science made them acutely aware of the importance of civil society mechanisms. There is more to society than just private firms and government bureaus.

## Civil Society Is a Real Thing

The intellectual background of Elinor Ostrom's account of how communities overcome tragedies of the commons rests with Vincent Ostrom's critique of the field of public administration (V. Ostrom 1973), in particular his critique of Wilson's progressivism, which led to the idea that (1) a government should be understood as a hierarchical organization with a single center of power, and (2) that all public problems required a government solution. In the Bloomington School account, both these ideas are fundamentally mistaken. As we have seen in the previous chapters, assumption A is seriously at odds with both the empirical reality of how governments actually operate, and with the quest for efficient governments (making government more hierarchical tends to make it less efficient). Assumption B is also mistaken, as private associations often address public issues, and often do it better than governments can.

In Vincent Ostrom's account, the "intellectual crisis" started when

> Wilson presumed that "there is always a centre of power." The burden of the analyst is to determine "the real depositaries and the essential machinery of power": "where in this system is that centre? In whose hands is self-sufficient authority lodged and through what agencies does that authority speak and act?" [Woodrow Wilson, *Congressional Government*, 1885]. Government is a process of command and control exercised from some supreme and self-sufficient center of authority. The State is an autonomous entity that rules over Society. (V. Ostrom 1997, 20)

Furthermore, the problem was then compounded when thinkers like John Dewey argued that, in a representative democracy, all public issues become the responsibility of the government:

> The search for the public turned into the discovery of the state. The public is those affected by the indirect consequences of human actions. These

indirect consequences are what economists might refer to as externalities or neighborhood effects. The agents responsible for the control of indirect consequences are officials—government. The state, then, in Dewey's inquiry, is conceptualized as both the government and the public as they interact with one another. The public acquires a consciousness of itself through the deliberations and actions taken by government. (V. Ostrom 1997, 41)

We can see this as a misguided attempt to simplify the complex reality of the public sphere. As Vincent Ostrom put it, Dewey should have titled his book *The Publics and Their Problems*, rather than *The Public and Its Problems*. "Dewey's warning about the abstractness and rigidity of 'concepts that are introduced by The,' applies to The Public as well as to The State. If he had been guided by his own warning, he could have carried his analyses much further." (V. Ostrom 1997, 43)

## The Hard Case: Common-Pool Resources

Let us start by considering the standard classification of the types of goods (V. Ostrom and Ostrom 1977) (Table 3.1). Going back to the simple examples given earlier, we can point out that two different types of common property actually exist. These two types are known as "public goods" and "common-pool resources" (CPRs). The pasture or the ocean fish stock are CPRs, while clean air or flood protection are public goods. They are both affected by the same kind of problem, namely by the difficulty to exclude people who damage the resource or free-ride. But they are different with respect to whether if one benefits from the resource, others can continue to benefit from it—what is known as rivalry in consumption. For instance, if one fisherman catches a fish, others can no longer have it; if one's sheep eat a patch of grass, less grass is left for other's sheep. By contrast, if I'm benefiting from clear air or flood protection, this does not subtract in any way from you benefiting from the same good. In other words, the joint consumption of flood protection poses no problems.

Because CPRs also suffer from a rivalry problem, they are the hardest case:

**Table 3.1.  Types of Goods**

|                   |      | Excludability |                      |
| ----------------- | ---- | ------------- | -------------------- |
|                   |      | *Easy*        | *Hard*               |
| Joint consumption | *Easy* | Club good   | Public good          |
|                   | *Hard* | Private good | Common-pool resource |

The dichotomy of pure public goods and private goods has become the focus of discussion about types of goods ... and consequently many have overlooked the other two types of goods that are created by this two-by-two typology: club goods are excludable but non-subtractable, and common-pool goods are difficult to exclude but subtractable. (Gibson, McKean, and E. Ostrom 2000, 6)

Neglecting club goods has led, as we will see below, to some misguided privatization policies, while "ignoring common-pool goods, which are difficult to exclude and easy to deplete, is tragic" (Gibson, McKean, and E. Ostrom 2000, 6):

> It turns out that most environmental and natural resources that we care about are common-pool goods. They are as subtractable as private goods, but because it is difficult to control or restrict access to them (the excludability dimension), it is very difficult to restrict the rate at which they are consumed. (Gibson, McKean, and E. Ostrom 2000, 6)

The main problem is that

> we arrive at a recognition of environmental crisis rather underequipped and ill accustomed to thinking about the crucial features of environmental resources. Because we have become accustomed to thinking in terms of only public goods and private goods, when we recognize that environmental resources are subtractable we begin to think of them as private goods. (Gibson, McKean, and E. Ostrom 2000, 6)

Interestingly, CPRs and public goods often come bundled together. For example, consider groundwater basins. These are large pools of underground water, with often uncertain boundaries and overall quantity. They usually span across many people's properties, and each person can tap into the groundwater basin by building wells (Elinor Ostrom 1965; Blomquist, Schlager, and Heikkila 2004; Schlager and Blomquist 2008). They get replenished thanks to surface rain sipping into the underground basin, with the soil acting as a filter—hence the relative purity of the water.

On one hand, the *quantity* of water available in a groundwater basin is a CPR—if one takes water from the underground basin, less water is left for others. If people take too much water, at a high rate, the natural replenishing rate may not be enough, eventually leaving everyone without water—a typical tragedy of the commons problem. Figure 3.2 shows the most vulnerable groundwater basins in the world according

Figure 3.2. Most Vulnerable Groundwater Basins Around the World. (Adapted from Richey, Thomas, Lo, Famiglietti, et al. 2015; Richey, Thomas, Lo, Reager, et al. 2015.)

to a recent NASA study which compared the natural replenishing rates to the extraction rates (Richey, Thomas, Lo, Famiglietti, et al. 2015; Richey, Thomas, Lo, Reager, et al. 2015).

On the other hand, the *quality* of the water in that groundwater basin is a public good—if one benefits from an unpolluted groundwater basin, others in no way benefit less from the same quality. The issue of quality is as important as the one of quantity, especially as groundwater basins have increasingly become affected by industrial pollution, which is not filtered properly by the soil (see Zachary A. Smith's chapter in Brentwood and Robar 2004).

In contrast to public goods or CPRs, private goods and club goods do not suffer from the excludability problem. We can see club goods as a method for the private provision of collective goods (Buchanan 1965, 1968; Demsetz 1970). Clubs include everything from homeowners associations to stock markets to Disneyland. If feasible methods for excluding noncontributors are devised, the tragedy of the commons can be solved by transforming public goods or CPRs into either private goods or club goods. This is why, as noted by Hardin, privatization is one possible solution to the tragedy of the commons. When possible, it will transform hard to exclude resources into easy to exclude resources. For instance, the solution that stock brokers developed to be safe from fraud was to set up the stock exchanges as clubs which excluded untrustworthy traders (Stringham 2015). Similarly, Disneyland is a large privately owned city providing everything from police protection to transport. By contrast, examples such as the Chinese "Great Leap Forward" illustrate what happens when the opposite is done—transforming a private good (privately owned farm land) into a CPR (collectivized farms), hence creating a tragedy of the commons where it didn't exist before. The example of ocean fish stock shows that CPRs may sometimes be very difficult or virtually impossible to privatize. Hardin's solution in such a case is to have a government agency create rules for preserving the resource and monitor people's behavior such that the rules are enforced. This corresponds to the idea that the government is the owner of the resource, in charge of creating and enforcing exclusion rules that would preserve the resource.

Innovative market solutions are sometimes created to deal with apparently impossible to solve public goods or CPR problems. For example, dangerous drivers create a public bad but it is difficult to exclude them from the roads. Nonetheless, an imperfect but viable mechanism does exist: dangerous driving tends to increase one's car insurance rate, and, hence, discourage such reckless driving. The free-riding problem with respect to paying for security is often solved by having a single owner of the land. For instance, shopping mall security is possible because the shopping mall is owned by a single legal entity which rents out spaces to individual shops. If the individual shops had individually owned the land, they would have faced a free-riding problem with respect to security, similar to the flood protection free-riding problem mentioned earlier. With a single owner of the land, the free-riding problem is avoided: the shopping mall hires the security, and the price of security is included in the rent that different shops pay to be part of the shopping mall.

While such solutions are sometimes possible, what Elinor Ostrom discovered was that privatization and government control were not the *only* possibilities, and in fact, while sometimes these standard solutions do work, in other cases they may actually underperform when compared to the neglected idea of self-governing communal solutions. This is highlighted by the title of her Nobel Prize address, "Beyond Markets and States" (Elinor Ostrom 2010a). In her Nobel Prize interview, she noted that after studying "several hundred irrigation systems in Nepal," they have discovered that "local groups are very effective" and that "farmer-managed irrigation systems are more effective in terms of getting water to the tail end, higher productivity, lower cost, than the fancy irrigation systems built with the help of Asian Development Bank, World Bank, USAID, etc." (Smith 2009). The farmers usually had much better knowledge of local conditions than outside governments and organizations, and a strong vested interest in solving the problem. One should not, however, overly idealize the capacity for self-governance: "we can't just now be naïve and think, 'Oh, well, just leave it to the people, they will always organize.' There are many settings that discourage self-organization" (Smith 2009). We will explore these conditions in more detail in the next chapter.

## WHAT ARE PROPERTY RIGHTS?

Interestingly, the theoretical foundation for Ostrom's discovery was being developed at about the same time that Hardin was writing his article, by two prominent University of California, Los Angeles (UCLA) economists, Harold Demsetz and Armen Alchian (Demsetz 1967; Alchian and Demsetz 1973).[1] At that same time, Elinor Ostrom was doing her PhD at

UCLA in the political science department, and she had earlier, in 1954, earned a BA from UCLA in political science. While an undergrad, she had actually studied economics with Armen Alchian, who was widely considered to have been a legendary teacher of economics. When I told this to Donald Boudreaux, an economics professor at George Mason University, he replied, "This explains a lot!" noting that he had always wondered how her economic analyses were always so good—better not just than those of a typical political scientist, but also of many economists.

## Property Is a Bundle of Rights

The theory developed by Demsetz and Alchian is known as the bundle of rights theory of property. E. Ostrom and her colleagues have made use of this theory as a way to map the complexities of commons problems (Schlager and Ostrom 1992; Hess and Ostrom 2006, 52–53; Elinor Ostrom 2010a). The key idea is that property is *not* a relationship between a thing and a person (or group), but a relationship between people *about* a thing. For instance, the fact that you own your car means that others are excluded from using it without your permission, and that you may do various things with your car (modify it, lease it, use it as a capital good, etc.).

Consider the right to exclude, which in some sense is the most fundamental aspect of property (Schmidtz 2000). How exactly it is enforced can differ, and, in practice, it is actually enforced in multiple complementary ways. The simplest form is purely private—you have a key to your car, while others don't. Social and legal aspects to exclusion complement this, first, in recognizing you as the rightful owner, and then in actually enforcing it. If your car is stolen, other people may provide information, and the police and the legal system may find it and punish the thief. In other cases, the governmental aspect may lack entirely, but property is still enforced by various collective mechanisms. For instance, in many parts of the world, farmers don't have legal formal titles to their land, but, within their villages, everyone knows who owns what piece of land, and the rights to land are enforced. The bottom line is that property is always about different people acknowledging each other's rights, in particular, the right to exclude others.

The right to exclude (or, more generally, manage) is not the only right included in the concept of property. A typical list of the rights in the bundle (Figure 3.3) includes the right to access, use, sell, inherit, rent,

*Chapter Three*

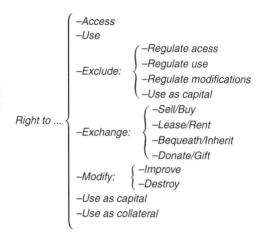

Figure 3.3.   Property as a Bundle of Rights.

change (improve or destroy), capital (ownership of what results from the use of the resource), and the right to use the property as collateral. This list of possible rights makes it possible to appreciate the diversity of "property rights regimes" (Schlager and Ostrom 1992). It is often the case that one doesn't have the entire list of rights, but only some of them.

Importantly, many contractual relationships can be understood as buying and selling of some of the rights in the bundle. For instance, when one rents an apartment one gets mainly the rights to access, use, and exclude. Some, but not all, leasing contracts also give one the right to sublease the apartment; but none of the other exchange rights (sell, bequeath, or donate).

Furthermore, consider the right to capital. Economists define "capital" as a good that produces a stream of income. For instance, a fisher's boat is a capital good, but the fish are not. The right to capital identifies who has the claim to the stream of income produced by the capital good. Some, but not all, leasing contracts give one the right to capital. Many firms rent, rather than own, their office spaces—which means that the owner of the space has granted the firm the right to use the space as capital. By contrast, consider a standard labor contract. When a worker uses various tools provided by the firm to make a product (e.g., build cars, extract oil, etc.), it is the firm, not the worker, that owns the end product. The firm may give the worker the right to exclude others from using "his" tools or office space, but not the right to capital. For instance, a biology professor at a university has "his or her" office space, has access to a laboratory, and the right to exclude others from "his or her" lab. The office space and lab are provided by the university, and, if the professor invents or discovers something, the university typically owns a large share of whatever patents the professor may obtain. In other words, the right to capital is (largely) kept by the university. To give another interesting example of the usefulness of the bundle of rights perspective, stock holders have the right to capital and exchange, but none of the others. For instance, if you own stock in a company, that does not grant you the right to access the company's factory floor or to directly intervene in its management.

We can see that many complex relationships involving property can be understood by thinking about which rights out of the bundle different people have. The broader point that Elinor Ostrom and others have made is that we can also use this perspective to understand not only contractual, commercial activities, but also social relations more generally. What is perceived as "legitimate" in one society or another depends on which rights people are assumed to have with respect to various goods.

In particular, we can use this conceptual framework to make sense of the different types of positions that people may have with respect to resources, including commonly owned property. Different positions, such as "owner," "proprietor," "claimant," "monitor," "authorized user" are defined by which rights they have out of the entire bundle (Table 3.2).

Table 3.2.    Bundles of Rights about Resources Define Different Types of Institutional Positions

|  | Owner | Proprietor | Claimant | Monitor | Authorized User |
|---|---|---|---|---|---|
| Access and use | ✓ | ✓ | ✓ | | ✓ |
| Modify | ✓ | ✓ | ✓ | | |
| Exclude | ✓ | ✓ | | ✓ | |
| Exchange | ✓ | | | | |

*Source*: Adapted from Schlager and Ostrom (1992).

## Self-Governance Depends on Mechanisms
## for Monitoring and Enforcing Rules

This type of analysis is essential for figuring out both (1) how groups of people self-govern, because they self-govern by creating various types of positions; and (2) the relationships between local communities and outside government. For instance,

> Turkish fishers who harvest from coastal lagoons are ... proprietors. The Turkish government leases lagoons to fishers' cooperatives. ... To access and harvest fish from the lagoon, a fisher must belong to the co-op. In order to belong to the co-op a fisher must reside in one of the three adjacent villages for at least six months and not have wage employment income. (Schlager and Ostrom 1992)

Although,

> the resource economics literature examining property rights and fishery regulation is generally pessimistic about the likelihood of fishers undertaking self-regulation so as to avoid inefficient economic outcomes ... an extensive empirical literature exists that documents a diversity of indigenous institutions devised by fishers without reference to governmental authorities ... Many of these de facto arrangements substantially reduce the incentives to overinvest in harvesting effort and to dissipate rent that fishers face in an open access fishery. Understanding the de facto arrangements that have enabled some fishers to reduce inefficient use of resources permits the development of better explanations of the conditions that inhibit or enhance effective self-organized collective solutions. (Schlager and Ostrom 1992)

The exact fashion in which people self-govern thus depends on their ingenuity in setting up institutional positions like those in Table 3.2, in a way that addresses effectively incentives and knowledge problems. A key issue is that of monitoring and enforcement. As mentioned in the introduction, rules need enforcement in order to be "in-use" rather than merely "in-form." But, in order for enforcement itself to be more than just "in-form," it seems that monitors also need monitoring. This seems to create a paradoxical infinite regress of monitors of monitors of monitors, etc. (Aligica and Tarko 2013, 2014c). At each layer of monitoring and enforcement, there exists a possibility of failure, either due to personal interests and opportunism of the parties involved, due to lack of legitimacy, or due to errors and lack of information. The more complicated the hierarchical system, the more inefficient overall monitoring and enforcement becomes. It is precisely for this reason that self-governing solutions are often more efficient than the government solutions. Pushing the problem of enforcement at higher and higher levels makes both information costs and the incentive problems worse. This means that solving the dilemma of enforcement by postulating a benevolent and informed third-party enforcer is usually not realistic. As Douglass North (1990, 55–56) has emphasized, "the dilemma that is posed by impersonal exchange without effective third-party enforcement is central to the major issues of development." Ostrom's solution to this dilemma is to look in the opposite direction, toward the details of local self-governance and polycentricity. Under what conditions do people successfully self-manage common-pool resources?

We can of course speculate, but Elinor Ostrom's approach was to first and foremost pay attention to a variety of empirical examples. For example, in a group of agents where the agents themselves take turns at being monitors, the self-interest problem is diminished to manageable levels because the monitor will now have a vested interest in making sure that the rules are followed. There's no longer a need to monitor the monitor. Even when the monitors are hired from outside the community, and the complexity of the system thus increases by involving more people, the monitors would still have the desire to uphold the rules in order to satisfy the demand of those who pay them. It is thus always important to consider the incentive structure of those responsible for rule design, monitoring, and enforcement. Examining numerous cases, we find that

> [m]ost long-surviving resource regimes select their own monitors, who are accountable to the appropriators or are appropriators themselves and who keep an eye on resource conditions as well as on harvesting activities…. The community creates an official position. In some systems appropriators rotate in this position so everyone has a duty to be a monitor. In other systems, all participants contribute resources and they jointly hire monitors. With local monitors, conditional operators are assured that someone is generally checking on the conformance of others to local rules. Thus, they can continue their own cooperation without constant fear that others are taking advantage of them. (Elinor Ostrom 2005a, 260–65)

## Why State Solutions Often Fail

People are not trapped in the tragedy of the commons. As they recognize that a better outcome is possible, they devise institutions to constrain each other and make sure individual incentives are harmonized with social cooperation. But, as noted by Elinor Ostrom, while such self-governing attempts do not always succeed, government attempts to "correct the game" also often fail. This is because "the advice to centralize control... is based on assumptions concerning the accuracy of information, monitoring capabilities, sanctioning reliability, and zero costs of administration" (Elinor Ostrom 1990, 10). These assumptions are often wrong. The incentives faced by external authorities are often not as good as those faced by local users who set up contracts among themselves and use mutually-agreed arbitrators:

> [T]he participants themselves design their own contracts... in light of the information they have at hand. The herders, who use the same meadow year after year, have detailed and relatively accurate information about carrying capacity. They observe the behavior of other herders and have incentives to report contractual infractions. Arbitrators may not need to hire monitors to observe the activities of the contracting parties. The self-interest of those who negotiated the contract will lead them to monitor each other and to report observed infractions so that the contract is enforced. (Elinor Ostrom 1990, 17)

By contrast,

> [a] regulatory agency, on the other hand, always needs to hire its own monitors. The regulatory agency then faces the principal–agent problem of how to ensure its monitors do their own job. The proponents of the central authority "solution" presume that such agencies have accurate information and are able to change incentives to [produce cooperation]. It is difficult for a central authority to have sufficient time-and-place information to estimate accurately both the carrying capacity of a CPR and the appropriate fines to induce cooperative behavior. I believe that situations... in which incomplete information leads to sanctioning errors occur more frequently than has been presumed in the policy literature. The need for external monitors and enforcers is particularly acute when what is being enforced is a decision by an external agent who may impose excess costs on participants. (Elinor Ostrom 1990, 17–18)

The alternative to "presuming that optimal institutional solutions can be designed easily and imposed at low costs by external authorities" is to bear in mind the "difficult, time-consuming, conflict-invoking process" of "getting the institutions right" (Elinor Ostrom 1990, 14). Moreover, as discussed earlier, "[s]ome enforcement mechanisms involve the users themselves as their own monitors" (p. 18), and it is thus a mistake to assume that "[w]hen the enforcement mechanism is not an external governmental agency … there is no enforcement" (p. 18).

## The Complexity and Limits of Private Property

Under what conditions could self-governance solutions retaining a common property regime be more efficient than private property regimes? Sometimes, private property is virtually impossible to create, as in the case of ocean fishing. I discuss some of these examples in more detail in the next chapter. Sometimes, however, private property may be relatively easy to implement, but it may, nonetheless, backfire.

An example of this is the privatization of land in India, which interfered with traditional transhumance practice to the detriment of animal herders and (sometimes) also farmers. Typically, the traditional relation between pastoralists and farmers was similar around the world. At the end of the harvest period, the herders will cross the fields, and the animal manure helps in fertilizing the land. Farmers do not thus have the incentive to try to exclude the pastoralists. More recently, conflicts between farmers and pastoralists have emerged partly because of the advent of chemical fertilizers, which reduced the need for the service provided by pastoralists, and partly because of the increased use of irrigation, which can be damaged by the herds passing over the fields. This means that the farmers now have the incentive to claim the land as solely theirs, and enforce a strict exclusion of pastoralists. The economists might think of various Coasian solutions (Coase 1960), according to which either the pastoralists would pay the farmers for damages or the farmers would bear the cost of, say, creating safe passages for the herds. Such solutions would diminish the conflict and internalize the cost that one party imposes upon the other. In practice, however, Indian farmers have greater political clout and governments have simply decided to side with the farmers at the expense of the pastoralists. (By contrast, in Nigeria the opposite is the case, with pastoralists having greater political clout, which has led to farmers having no recourse when their crops are destroyed by cow herds.) This is an example in which the creation of private property with strict exclusion rights has increased conflict and disproportionately harmed one party, rather than facilitating cooperation. Part of the problem here is that the intervention of the outside government can be used as a substitute to finding endogenous Coasian solutions.

A very different type of example concerns the privatization of forests. At first glance, forests may seem like an easy and obvious case for privatization: "Private property arrangements win praise and admiration, appropriately, because they encourage protection and investment in the goods to which they attach" (Gibson, McKean, and E. Ostrom 2000, 6). Forests do not seem to suffer from exclusion difficulties in the same way that ocean fish do. However, forests actually provide more than just wood, and "[t]he size of many forests, and the inevitable complications involved in monitoring the use of the forest and balancing one use against the other, make exclusion or restrictions on access intrinsically problematic" (Gibson, McKean, and E. Ostrom 2000, 7). Many economists underestimate this complexity by thinking that they are "the source of only one commodity, wood," and by neglecting the diversity of groups with divergent interests with respect to the forests (Gibson, McKean, and E. Ostrom 2000, 5). By contrast, the reality is that "forests are associated with *multiple products* (for example, wood for construction and fuel, wildlife, water, leaves, fruits, fodder, straw, shade, fertile soil, stones, and so on) and *multiple user groups* (defined by property rights, product, location, citizenship, religion, caste, ethnicity, technology, income, and access)" (p. 5). Furthermore, "[t]hey also provide environmental services beyond the forest, in terms of erosion control, flood control, conservation of water, cleaning air and water, and stabilization of local climate" (p. 7).

Margaret McKean has identified several general conditions under which privatization tends to be an inferior strategy to communal self-governance (p. 8):

1. "some resources are intrinsically indivisible." This is the case with typical public goods like flood protection, but it also fits cases in which "forests contain and produce useful items that are themselves fugitive or mobile resources." Birds and wild animals in forests and fish in the ocean are good examples.
2. "there is great uncertainty in the location from year to year of the most productive zones." Ocean fish are again a good example. They are not just highly mobile, but the precise areas where they gather can change from year to year in unpredictable ways.
3. When the resource has multiple possible uses and it faces "competing uses and high population pressure" and, hence, "coordination among users is essential to cope with externalities." This is

often the case with collective goods within cities, but, more generally, it applies to all cases when the transaction costs of settling the disputes created by externalities are too high. Splitting the property into many small properties increases such transaction costs.
4. When the costs on monitoring and enforcement become prohibitive, either because many people can either free-ride or overuse the resource, or because the physical conditions make monitoring difficult. For example river deltas may suffer from such problems due to their relative wilderness. Under such conditions, the solution is to enhance the vested interest in the resource of all the members of the community: "group ownership and thus group enforcement of rules can be an efficient way to cope with the costs of monitoring otherwise porous boundaries and enforcing restraints on use within those boundaries."

To make matters worse, even when private property could in principle provide a proper solution, governments often pursue privatization as a top-down strategy, while misunderstanding the subtleties of private property arrangements, in particular, the feasibility of club-like arrangements. The biggest misconception about private property is that it necessarily involves *individual* ownership. As shown by examples such as joint-stock companies and other corporations, it is often desirable to have multiple owners of a private enterprise (see Kuran 2005; Leeson 2014; Stringham 2015). Not understanding this, most "campaigns to create private property rights tend to consist of transferring ownership from larger entities and groups to individuals.... Most privatization campaigns would ignore or even oppose the assertion that there may be conditions when it is more desirable for clear, specific, secure, and exclusive rights to be vested in a group rather than in single individuals" (Gibson, McKean, and E. Ostrom 2000, 7). This strategy can easily backfire when "these interventions may destroy the property-rights arrangements that they should want most to create" (p. 7), especially by heightening problem 4 mentioned above, regarding monitoring and enforcement.

We can understand this as a trade-off between the costs and benefits of inclusion (Figure 3.4). The strategy to try to privatize everything to individual level ignores the marginal benefits curve and only pays attention to the increase in collective action problems such as the possibility of free-riding. For instance, this trade-off determines whether a company decides to go public and how many shares to issue. Going

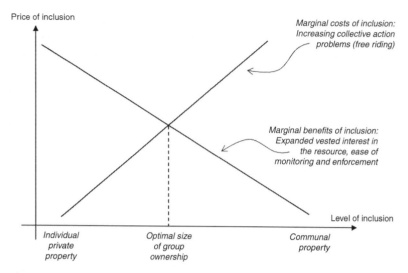

Price of inclusion

Marginal costs of inclusion:
Increasing collective action
problems (free riding)

Marginal benefits of inclusion:
Expanded vested interest in
the resource, ease of
monitoring and enforcement

Level of inclusion

Individual
private
property

Optimal size
of group
ownership

Communal
property

**Figure 3.4.    Costs and Benefits of Inclusion.**

public has the benefit of attracting more capital (inclusion), but has the cost of diminishing the decision-making control that the original owners and founders of the company have. The same logic applies much more generally, and assuming that private property is necessarily individual, rather than club-like, can lead to serious public policy errors by hampering various parties from capturing the benefits of inclusion in larger clubs.

## Summary

It is thus important to bear in mind (1) which property-rights arrangement is best suited for the nature of the resource, and (2) the complexity of any given "type" of property.

Consider point (1) first. As noted by Gibson, McKean, and E. Ostrom, "[i]t is widely agreed that private property rights are the appropriate institution to create for commodities that are subtractable and from which it is easy to exclude others from benefits. Thus, if one thinks of natural resource systems as potentially private goods, one will advocate creating private property rights for these resources" (2000, 7). By contrast, if one understands that "natural-resource systems ... are really combinations of public goods and common-pool goods," one is lead to the conclusion that "vesting property rights in groups [may be] more efficient than vesting those rights either in a single individual or trying to parcel the resource into individually titled parcels" (Gibson, McKean, and E. Ostrom 2000, 7–8).

Point (2) is also extremely important. For instance, "if one's notion of private property rights requires vesting all such rights in individuals, then one will fail to consider the possibility of vesting rights in groups or communities when that might be appropriate" (Gibson, McKean, and E. Ostrom 2000, 7). As mentioned, "private property" itself covers a complex array of possibilities ranging from the simple individual ownership (in which all the rights in the Figure 3.3 bundle are vested in a single person) all the way to highly complex corporate and club arrangements. All such arrangements are classified as "private property" because they are ultimately reducible to contractual relations between individuals.

Alternatives to private property involve more than just contracts, namely the use of more or less explicit social norms and rules, in the case of communal self-governing arrangements or the use of government controls and management, in case of government-owned resources. As we'll see in more detail in the next chapter, common-property arrangements also cover many possible institutional arrangements, and the key problem is to identify the basic principles that favor productive resource management.

These distinctions among private, communal, and government property are to some extent idealized, as they cannot be fully separated. Social norms and government regulations are involved to some extent in the enforcement of private property contractual relations, and government management of resources often relies upon social norms and is complemented by private governance. Nonetheless, despite being somewhat idealized, they are still useful conceptual distinctions.

## BOTTOM-UP SOLUTIONS TO SOCIAL DILEMMAS

Let us now look more closely at the mathematical structure underpinning all examples of the "tragedy of the commons," and Elinor Ostrom's fundamental theoretical insight that the structure of the game is not fixed, because the agents themselves can endogenously alter the game's payoffs. Here in a nutshell is the methodological underpinning

**Table 3.3.   Engineering Cooperation by Punishing Defectors**

**(a) Relatively mild punishment**

Prisoners' Dilemma

| | | Person 2 | |
|---|---|---|---|
| | | Cooperates | Defects |
| Person 1 | Cooperates | 7 \ 7 | 0 \ **10** |
| | Defects | **10** \ 0 | 5 \ 5 |

→

Stag Hunt

| | | Person 2 | |
|---|---|---|---|
| | | Cooperates | Defects |
| Person 1 | Cooperates | **7** \ 7 | 0 \ 5 |
| | Defects | 5 \ 0 | 5 \ 5 |

**(b) Harsh punishment**

Prisoners' Dilemma

| | | Person 2 | |
|---|---|---|---|
| | | Cooperates | Defects |
| Person 1 | Cooperates | 7 \ 7 | 0 \ **10** |
| | Defects | **10** \ 0 | 5 \ 5 |

→

Coordination Game

| | | Person 2 | |
|---|---|---|---|
| | | Cooperates | Defects |
| Person 1 | Cooperates | **7** \ 7 | 0 \ **0** |
| | Defects | 5 \ 0 | 5 \ 5 |

of her approach, the set of basic assumptions about human beings that frames her understanding of social dilemmas:

> As an institutionalist studying empirical phenomena, I presume that individuals try to solve problems as effectively as they can. That assumption imposes a discipline on me. Instead of presuming that some individuals are incompetent, evil, or irrational and others are omniscient, I presume that individuals have similar limited capabilities to reason and figure out the structure of complex environments. It is my responsibility as a scientist to ascertain what problems individuals are trying to solve and what factors help or hinder them in these efforts. When the problems that I observe involve lack of predictability, information and trust, as well as high levels of complexity and transactional difficulties, then my efforts to explain must take these problems overtly into account rather than assuming them away. In developing an explanation for observed behavior, I draw on a rich literature written by other scholars interested in institutions and their effects on individual incentives and behavior in field settings. (Elinor Ostrom 1990, 26)

The game theoretical approach helps us see how "individuals try to solve problems as effectively as they can." Game theory is a generalization of basic utility theory. In utility theory, it is assumed that each possible choice corresponds to a particular subjective benefit for the individual. People are subjected to constraints that limit their set of possible choices, but, within those constraints, they choose whatever brings them the highest benefit. The main approximation in utility theory is that it assumes that the benefits that one person gets from a particular choice is not influenced by other people's choices. For example, when you decide what groceries to buy, you care mainly about your direct preference, not about what other people buy. But, in many cases, you cannot ignore what others are doing because their choices may limit your choices. Game theory lifts this conceptual limitation, focusing instead precisely on how the benefit that one gets from a given choice is affected by the choices made by others. As such, people are now assumed to try to maximize their benefits conditional on their assumptions about what others will do (Aumann 1987).

Importantly, game theory allows us to make sense of "perverse spontaneous orders" (V. H. Storr and Storr 2008), that is, cases in which when everyone maximizes their own expected benefit the overall aggregate results are less than optimal (according to the participants

*Solution of non-cooperative game, no benefit to change*

themselves). The game theoretical concept of "Nash equilibrium" identifies the aggregate result of individual choices. This equilibrium is reached when no one has the incentive to change their choice.

## From Prisoners' Dilemma to the Stag Hunt

Let us first consider one of the most famous games, the Prisoners' Dilemma, which also happens to provide the mathematical structure of the tragedy of the commons. In the simplest version of this game, there are only two participants, and each has the choice to either cooperate or defect. If they both choose to cooperate they each get a higher individual benefit than if they both choose to defect. In Table 3.3, left panel, this is reflected by the fact that for mutual cooperation each player gets a benefit of 7, while for mutual defection they each get a benefit of 5. For example, the two people may be two shepherds sharing the same pasture. They cooperate if they choose to limit the number of sheep such that the pasture is not overgrazed. By contrast, they defect if they choose to have too many sheep, and the pasture is overgrazed. They both prefer that the pasture is not overgrazed. However, if one of them decides to cooperate, while the other defects, the one that cooperates gets the lowest possible benefit. The pasture may not be completely overgrazed, but it is still not used sustainably. So the cooperative shepherd gets the downside of having fewer sheep (and thus lower profits from them) *and* the downside of a poorer pasture. By contrast, the defector now has the advantage of earning the profits from having many sheep *and* the benefit of not having to cope with a totally overgrazed pasture. In this case, the cooperator gets the worst possible deal, while the defector gets the best.

What makes the situation difficult is the fact that both shepherds, assuming they're not stupid, will think as follows: If the other guy decides to have fewer sheep (cooperates), I can get the best deal by defecting; but if the other guy decides to defect, I'd better defect as well so at least I get the high profits while the pasture lasts. In other words, regardless of the other person's choice, the best choice is for you to defect. This is why the equilibrium is the shaded cell in Table 3.3, corresponding to mutual defection. But notice that both shepherds are dissatisfied with this result! According to their own values, they would've been better off if they, somehow, had managed to cooperate. But the logic of the situation traps them in the inefficient situation.

Before Elinor Ostrom, this is where the analysis would have stopped—drawing the conclusion that the parties in the Prisoners' Dilemma are doomed to experience the tragedy of the commons. But that is wrong:

> What makes these models so interesting and so powerful is that they capture important aspects of many different problems that occur in the world. What makes these models so dangerous—when they are used metaphorically as the foundation of policy—is that the constraints that are assumed to be fixed for the purpose of analysis are taken on faith as being fixed in empirical settings, unless external authorities change them.... Not all users of natural resources are ... incapable of changing their constraints. As long as individuals are viewed as prisoners, policy prescriptions will address this metaphor. I would rather address the question of how to enhance the capabilities of those involved to change the constraining rules of the game to lead to outcomes other than remorseless tragedies. (Elinor Ostrom 1990, 6–7)

Imagine that the participants look at the left panel in Table 3.3, and they notice that 7 is better than 5—they *understand* that mutual cooperation would be preferable to the current equilibrium of mutual defection. And they are not helpless. They can use their understanding of why they end up in the "perverse spontaneous order" to devise rules for escaping it. Tables 3.3 and 3.4 show two such possibilities (in bold are the payoffs that are changed). They can either implement rules that punish defection or they may have rules to reward cooperation. Relatively mild punishments, as well as the rewards, transform the game from a Prisoners' Dilemma to a Stag Hunt—a game that has two possible equilibria, including mutual cooperation.

We have pretty good evidence that it is the Stag Hunt, rather than the Prisoners' Dilemma, that actually characterizes most social situations (Skyrms 2003; Tomasello 2009). Harsher punishments lead to what is known as a Coordination Game, which also has two equilibria just like the Stag Hunt. The Coordination Game is relevant for understanding how people exit conflict situations, and the importance of social–political entrepreneurs for turning mutual cooperation into a "focal point" (Coyne 2008, chap. 2; more on this in Chapter 5).

The Stag Hunt is usually described with the following metaphor. Suppose that two hunter-gatherers decide to hunt a stag. Catching a stag is difficult and no one can do it just by themselves. They need to

**Table 3.4.  Engineering Cooperation by Rewarding Cooperation**

*Prisoners' Dilemma*

| | | Person 2 | |
|---|---|---|---|
| | | *Cooperates* | *Defects* |
| Person 1 | Cooperates | 7 / 7 | 0 / 10 |
| | Defects | 10 / 0 | 5 / 5 |

→

*Stag Hunt*

| | | Person 2 | |
|---|---|---|---|
| | | *Cooperates* | *Defects* |
| Person 1 | Cooperates | **15** / **15** | 0 / 10 |
| | Defects | 10 / 0 | 5 / 5 |

cooperate to catch it. However, while in the forest trying to hunt the stag, one may get tempted to try something easier such as catching a rabbit. So, a situation of mutual cooperation corresponds to the case in which the two work together to catch the stag, a situation of mutual defection corresponds to when they both catch a rabbit. Unlike the case of a Prisoners' Dilemma, when one gets the highest payoff when they defect and the other cooperates, in the Stag Hunt there's no particular benefit from tricking the other. When one catches the rabbit while the other is left out as a fool trying to catch the stag, one gets the same payoff as when they both go for the rabbits. Because of this, there is no incentive to move away from the mutual cooperation situation.

The mathematics of this game leads to the conclusion that the two people will cooperate as long as they trust each other. In other words, if one thinks it is likely that the other person cooperates, one's best option is to also cooperate. Only if one thinks the other person is likely to defect (and go for the rabbit), is defection an attractive choice. Once again, this is very different from the Prisoners' Dilemma, where *regardless* of what you think the other is going to do, your best option is always to defect.

The details of how exactly the parties will decide to punish defection or reward cooperation are obviously important. It is those details that make it difficult to simply take one institution from one place and implement it in another. One interesting and particularly important case involves escaping the Prisoners' Dilemma thanks to repeated interactions (Axelrod 1984, 1997). Suppose the game is played again and again, indefinitely. If one defects in one round of the game, the other player may defect in retribution in the next rounds. What matters in the repeated game is not so much the outcome in one single round, but the aggregate outcome over time. If players use so-called trigger strategies, such as holding a grudge and always defecting after being stood up once, the aggregated many-rounds Prisoners' Dilemma can actually transform into a Stag Hunt. This is why people take so much trouble to establish good reputations, and build institutions that use reputations (Stringham 2015).

## Beyond the Prisoners' Dilemma Model

The tragedy of commons, as modeled by the Prisoners' Dilemma, is just one example among many of possible social dilemmas. There are other

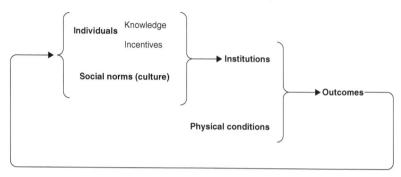

**Figure 3.5.   Endogenous Institutional Change. (Adapted from Gibson, McKean, and E. Ostrom 2000, 9: fig. 1.1.)**

possible "perverse spontaneous orders." For example, in his account of the origins of social institutions, Andrew Schotter lists three more types of social dilemmas, apart from tragedy of the commons (included in Cowen 1992, chap. 8): coordination problems, inequality-preserving problems, and cooperation problems. More recently, Bryan Bruns has catalogued the topology of *all* 2-players-2-choices possible games, which gives a broad metaperspective on games stability (Bruns 2012, 2015). Based on this, we can now think not just about equilibrium *within* a given game, but also about equilibrium *across* games—that is, which games do participants want to change? In the analysis above, Prisoners' Dilemma is not a stable game, as people want to escape it, and often succeed in crafting rules for doing so. By contrast, the Stag Hunt or the Coordination Game are more stable—if participants succeed in building trust or finding a good focal point for coordination, and, thus, succeed in reaching the productive equilibrium within the game, they do not have the incentive to further change the game. In that sense, the institutions that preserve the Stag Hunt or the Coordination Game are *self-enforcing*, that is, people have a vested interest in preserving them.

The logic of endogenous institutional change described by Elinor Ostrom applies to all such cases. In Chapter 5 we will return to this issue from the perspective of social–political entrepreneurship and what is known as the Institutional Analysis and Development (IAD) framework. But for now, let us just give a very broad summary of this logic (Figure 3.5). Influenced by their culture, and building upon their knowledge and self-interest, individuals support certain institutions, including monitoring and enforcing rules. Depending on the nature of the resource, these institutions may work more or less well. Based on the observed outcomes, the individuals learn, and, hence, change the institutions to some extent (Tarko 2015c). Observed outcomes (either positive or negative) may also affect the local culture by legitimizing or delegitimizing certain ways of interacting.

## NOTE

1. Harold Demsetz (1970) has also been very critical of Paul Samuelson's (1954) theory of public goods, building on James Buchanan's (1968) book, *The Demand and Supply of Public Goods*, which has also been a major influence upon the Bloomington School. Samuelson's (1954) theory has also been attacked from a different direction by Tiebout's (1956) theory of institutional competition, which has led to the broader theory of polycentricity (V. Ostrom, Tiebout, and Warren 1961). For a collection of some of the key articles in the public goods debate, see Cowen (1992).

# Chapter Four

# Resilience

## Understanding the Institutional Capacity to Cope with Shocks and Other Challenges

When we change policy—when we add a rule, change a rule, or adopt some new set of rules—we are in effect running an experiment based on more or less informed expectations about the likely outcome.... The need to experiment and the chance that we're going to make mistakes alerts us to the positive side of redundancy and multiple, parallel jurisdictions. In any design process that involves a substantial probability of error, using redundant teams of designers has been shown as one way of reducing the costs of big mistakes. If there are multiple jurisdictions with considerable autonomy at the local level, policy makers can experiment more or less simultaneously within their separate jurisdictions.... [B]ecause polycentric systems have overlapping units, information about what has worked well in one setting can be transmitted to other units. And when small systems fail, there are larger systems to call upon—and vice versa. (Elinor Ostrom, interviewed by Aligica 2003)

On January 12, 2010, a massive magnitude-7.0 earthquake hit Haiti. The earthquake released the equivalent energy of 32 Hiroshima bombs or 65,000 average hurricanes hitting all at once. More than 100,000 people died.[1] A cholera outbreak followed, killing more than 9,000 people, and affecting around 6% of Haiti's population. The infrastructure was largely destroyed making aid and rescue attempts more difficult. Recovery was difficult, and the Haiti earthquake has left a mark that is still strongly felt to this day.

On February 27 of the same year, a magnitude-8.8 earthquake hit Chile. This earthquake was 500 times more powerful than the one in

Photo 5.  *Vincent Ostrom, Tej Kumari Mahat (Chair Person of the FMIS in Sera-baguwa bandh Irrigation System), and Elinor Ostrom in Tharpu village, Tanahu, January 1992 (Arizona State University, 1993).*

Haiti, the equivalent of almost 16,000 Hiroshima bombs dropped all at once. And yet, "only" a few hundred people died in Chile. The recovery from the damage was also swift and efficient.

What accounts for such a massive difference between Haiti and Chile (Lovett 2010)? The proximate factors, such as good building codes and a relatively effective government, provide only the starting point for answering this question. One of the main contributions of

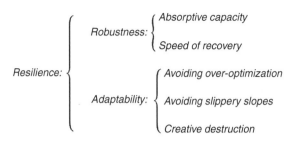

**Figure 4.1. The Defining Characteristics of Resilience.**

Elinor Ostrom and her collaborators on the topic of *resilience* has been to look beyond such proximate factors, explaining how *institutional background* helps or hinders long-term preparedness (McGinnis 1999a; Elinor Ostrom 2005a, chap. 9; Toonen 2010; Aligica and Tarko 2014c).

We can structure our thinking about resilience in several steps going from a simple perspective to a complex one (Figure 4.1). Let us explore each of these elements in more detail.

## CONCEPTUALIZING RESILIENCE

### An Equilibrium Perspective

The simplest perspective on resilience is sometimes referred to as "robustness" (Adger 2006). This refers, first of all, to the capacity of the system to experience a large shock without major negative consequences—what is known as "absorptive capacity." For example, in the Haiti–Chile earthquake comparison, Chile's infrastructure had a much higher absorption capacity than Haiti's. Some of the recent literature on resilience is focused on how structural factors such as population density and heterogeneity help "push a system far away from [its] critical points, helping the system to sustain large perturbations" Gao, Barzel, and Barabási 2016).

Another aspect of robustness refers to the speed of recovery. Even if the shock had a large initial impact, some systems recover quicker than other. For example, different counties recovered at very different speeds from Hurricane Katrina, which is explained by the preexisting (and largely informal) institutional structure ( Chamlee-Wright 2013; Grube and Storr 2013; N. M. Storr, Chamlee-Wright, and Storr 2015).

This perspective on robustness provides only a static, equilibrium approach. Most problematically, it assumes that it is desirable for the system to return to the same state of affairs it has had before the shock. But this may not be true. The vulnerability to the shock may have revealed a design error. For example, the new information from a shock like an earthquake, a hurricane, or a flooding may lead to different relative insurance rates across different geographical areas, which, in turn, will determine a recovery to a different state of affairs. The important idea is that the same logic also applies more broadly to institutional design errors. The concept of "adaptability" (Gunderson 2000; Folke et al. 2002) captures this intuition about the importance of learning, while opening the door for a more sophisticated analysis of resilience. Such an analysis needs to account for overoptimization problems, for possible slippery slopes, while allowing entrepreneurship and "creative destruction" to persist.

## Highly Optimized Tolerance

The most important resilience problem that adaptive systems can suffer from is overoptimization. The mathematical theory was developed by Carlson and Doyle (1999, 2000, 2002; Zhou, Carlson, and Doyle 2005), who refer to the problem of "highly-optimized tolerance" (HOT), and the idea was later adopted by Elinor Ostrom and her collaborators as a basis for their theory of ecological resilience (Janssen, Anderies, and Ostrom 2004, 2007; Anderies and Janssen 2013; Elinor Ostrom 2014). Carlson and Doyle have demonstrated a striking mathematical phenomenon: optimization to cope with past shocks can itself create *previously inexistent* vulnerabilities with respect to other, unforeseen sources of uncertainty. As a result of optimization, we obtain a system that is characterized by "(1) high efficiency, performance, and robustness to designed-for uncertainties; (2) hypersensitivity to design flaws and unanticipated perturbations; (3) nongeneric, specialized, structured configurations; and (4) power laws" (Carlson and Doyle 1999, 1423). The system is "robust-yet-fragile": As it is optimized to the *known* sources of danger, the system develops, as a side effect, weak points thanks to complex interconnectivities, which open up the possibility of "cascading spread of damage due to the seemingly innocuous breakdown of individual parts" (Carlson and Doyle 2002, 2540).

The importance of this problem can hardly be overstated. As Carlson and Doyle (1999, 1424) put it, "the most important feature of HOT states is the fact that the high performance and robustness of optimized designs with respect to the uncertainty for which they were designed [i.e., in economic parlance, risk], is accompanied by extreme sensitivity to additional uncertainty that is not included in the design." This leads to "profound tradeoffs in robustness and uncertainty" and to the conclusion that "there are fundamental limitations that can be viewed as 'conservation principles.'"

Consider one of the classic examples of this problem. During the 1950s and 1960s, the pulp and paper industry in eastern Canada was suffering from trees being infested with the spruce budworm (a serious pest of conifers). In reaction to this, they used insecticide, which significantly reduced the problem. This made many more trees available for the pulp and paper industry and "encouraged expansion of pulp mills but left the forest, and hence, the economy, more vulnerable to an outbreak that would cause more intense and more extensive tree mortality than had ever been experienced before" (Holling 1996, 37). In other words, the very solution to the problem increased vulnerability, partly because "protected foliage...became more homogenous over larger areas, demanding ever more vigilance and control" (Holling 1996, 37).

## The Problem of Self-Interested Actors Evading Rules

When people are involved, the problem of overoptimization can become even worse. Regulations often create incentives for people to discover regulatory *evasions*, which basically render obsolete the robustness calculations that formed the basis for setting up the regulations in the first place. Elinor Ostrom has highlighted this problem as crucial for properly understanding how to design a resilient system: "As soon as one design has proved itself in one environment, innovations in strategies adopted by participants or changes in the environment in which humanly designed system is in operation will produce unexpected results" (Elinor Ostrom 2005a, 255). As such, simple equilibrium analysis "can be difficult to apply to systems in which some components are consciously designed" and one has to consider the "*endogenous processes* within a given system of interest and...address normative considerations associated with incentives and decisions" (Anderies and Janssen 2013, emphasis added).

Elinor Ostrom encountered this problem early on in the study of local public economies. For instance, as mentioned earlier, her introduction to *The Delivery of Urban Services* book, that she edited, starts out by highlighting this very issue:

> [F]ar too many urban programs are based on inadequate analysis of how institutional arrangements affect the strategic considerations of various participants. Surprising and frequently tragic results have followed. Failure, in many cases, leads to adoption of another program—one often based, as was the first, on inadequate analysis of the strategic behavior of the different actors. Failure seems to breed failure. (Elinor Ostrom 1976b, 7)

The concern about how to create rules that curtail people's antisocial opportunistic acts runs through her entire work, an aspect that she shared with her Nobel corecipient, Oliver Williamson. But while Williamson studied the problem of opportunism in organizations and interfirm relations, Elinor Ostrom studied it in the context of larger scale social norms and formal institutions.

The more complex the system, the more serious this problem becomes because our ability to predict and control how the system works by means of various top-down regulations sharply diminishes. Regulatory evasion is not the end of the story. When we look at the problem from the point of view of the highly optimize tolerance idea, we see that the spiral of regulatory complexity and regulatory evasion can generate previously inexistent vulnerabilities, and make matters worse.

## Polycentricity as a Method to Design Resilient Systems

The only way to avoid the problem of highly optimized tolerance is to decentralize the system such that we create "small isolated clusters that would be highly robust to changes in probability distributions or flaws" (Carlson and Doyle 1999, 1423). As Carlson and Doyle point out, such a solution to the resilience problem is deliberately inefficient in terms of economies of scale. However, the only way in which a complex system can be made resilient is by giving up the goal of maximum short-term efficiency, keeping the scale low, and implementing redundancies. The emphasis on polycentricity, a system of governance comprised of many decision centers, in which "[e]ach unit exercises considerable independence to make and enforce rules within a circumscribed domain of authority" (Elinor Ostrom 2005a, 283), and on diversity, that is, pre-serving a redundant variety of institutional devices rather than adopting a one-size-fits-all solution, should be understood from this perspective that stresses the importance of coping with uncertainty, rather than just risk.

Elinor Ostrom and her collaborators have indeed taken this to be a resilience argument in favor of polycentricity. The polycentric alterna-tive is more resilient because, on one hand, due to "overlapping units, information about what has worked well in one setting can be transmit-ted to others who may try it out in their settings," and, on the other hand, "when small systems fail, there are larger systems to call upon—and vice versa" (Elinor Ostrom 2005a, 283). She concludes that "[t]he important point is: If the systems are relatively separable, allocating responsibility for experimenting with rules will not avoid failure, but will drastically reduce the probability of immense failures for an entire region" (p. 284).

But would such a polycentric system also suffer from overoptimiza-tion? Miller and Page (2007, 139) note that "[a]daptive systems have to deal with the tension between the benefits of achieving precise behavior and the cost of increased system fragility." Overly detailed systems of rules, attempting to provide a precise and "optimal" answer to every possible situation, are less robust "because the structures necessary for delicate behavior require an underlying system that is rich in possibili-ties. In essence, we need a quivering system that will fall into the right state with only a gentle tap. In such a system, an improper tap can lead to very unpredictable results" (Miller and Page 2007, 139). The more precise one attempts to control everything by devising overly specific and optimized rules, the larger the number of variables unavoidably becomes. The space of possibilities becomes larger, and, hence, the probability of error increases and the system's robustness to unpredict-able shocks, that is, its ability of resisting something more than just a "gentle tap," becomes smaller.

Miller and Page argue that self-organizing adaptive social systems tend toward relatively simple systems of rules which "are likely to be easier to find and maintain" (p. 140). Nonetheless, simple systems might gradually evolve toward more complicated ones "if we assume that there is an adaptive path from one to the other" (p. 140). The HOT process describes this path. However, Miller and Page also point out that in polycentric systems there is a limit to the complexity that can be arrived at by bottom-up gradual adaptations because natural selection tends to create risk-adverse decision-centers. Over the long term, decision-centers that are not sufficiently risk-adverse sooner or later break down due to some unpredictable shock. Only the risk-adverse systems survive over the long term. This is why the resilience of self-regulation tends to be less of a problem and less vulnerable to the HOT problem. However, when rules are devised in a top-down fashion, this opens the door for greater fragility into the system.

Elinor Ostrom was confronted with the importance of these ideas right from the start, as she was analyzing the success and failures of local public economies. But the same idea about the importance of polycentricity as a mechanism for creating resilient systems has popped up again and again throughout her entire career. Here's how she described the issue in the introduction to *The Delivery of Urban Services* book, emphasizing the "growing possibility of developing a cumulative, empirical theory of institutional analysis and design":

> The wide range of institutional arrangements found in America's metropolitan areas is seen as an asset. Reliance on any single set of decision rules exposes all to the risk of total institutional failure. In an imperfect world where institutions are filled with weaknesses, redundancy in organizational arrangements may prevent the failure of any one set of decision rules from seriously handicapping us, as citizens, in accomplishing some of our goals. Multiplicity of arrangements also enables us to test the relative performance of different types of institutional practices and thus evolve new solutions to different kind of problems. (Elinor Ostrom 1976b, 8)

## Avoiding Slippery Slopes

The problem of slippery slopes is arguably the most difficult theoretically, and, yet, it cannot be ignored (Walker et al. 2004; Diamond 2005). A resilient system has the "ability to avoid slippery slopes towards catastrophic thresholds," where a threshold is defined as a point toward which "[t]he society can move … without significant losses in its standard of living and yet, once the threshold is reached, degradation becomes rapid, profound and hard to stop" (Aligica and Tarko 2014c).

A classic example of a slippery slope is the standard story of the Easter Island, where a fairly advanced society collapsed as the inhabitants of the island gradually cut down all the trees. As Jared Diamond put it, "Easter Islanders surely wouldn't have been so foolish as to cut down all their trees, when the consequences would have been so obvious to them. ... I have often asked myself, 'What did the Easter Islander who cut down the last palm tree say while he was doing it?'" (Diamond 2005, 114). The answer is that when enough of them realized the consequences, it was already too late for them to organize a proper response. The threshold had already been passed. The Easter Island collapse is both spectacular and unique:

> [T]he Pacific encompasses thousands of inhabited islands, almost all of whose inhabitants were chopping down trees, clearing gardens, burning firewood, building canoes, and using wood and rope for houses and other things. Yet, among all those islands, only three in the Hawaiian Archipelago, all of them much drier than Easter—the two islets of Necker and Nihoa, and the larger island of Niihau—even approach Easter in degree of deforestation. (Diamond 2005, 115)

Diamond argues that this collapse was due to a combination of ecological conditions, "they had the misfortune to be living in one of the most fragile environments, at the highest risk for deforestation, of any Pacific people" (p. 118), and the internal sociopolitical dynamic, in which rivaling societies were caught in a Prisoners' Dilemma competition which led to the unintended outcome:

> Both oral traditions preserved by the islanders, and archaeological surveys, suggest that Easter's land surface was divided into about a dozen (either 11 or 12) territories, each belonging to one clan or lineage group, and each starting from the seacoast and extending inland—as if Easter were a pie cut into a dozen radial wedges. Each territory had its own chief and its own major ceremonial platforms supporting statues. The clans competed peacefully by seeking to outdo each other in building platforms and statues, but eventually their competition took the form of ferocious fighting. That division into radially sliced territories is typical for Polynesian islands elsewhere in the Pacific. What is unusual in that respect about Easter is that, again according to both oral traditions and archaeological surveys, those competing clan territories were also integrated religiously, and to some extent economically and politically, under the leadership of one paramount chief. (Diamond 2005, 94)

Polycentricity is defined as a system of independent decision-centers operating under an overarching system of rules. In the Easter Island example, it was the lack of proper overarching rules that ultimately caused the collapse. As shown by Elinor Ostrom (1990), and as we have seen in the previous chapter, people often do escape Prisoners' Dilemmas, but they do so only under certain conditions. In the case of Easter Island, the "leadership of one paramount chief" has failed to deliver the proper large-scale coordination and foresight.

This problem of slippery slopes is currently on the agenda especially with respect to global environmental problems (Buck 1998; Elinor Ostrom 1999b; Elinor Ostrom 2010b). What makes the problem so difficult is, on one hand, the transaction costs involved in reaching an agreement between so many countries, and, on the other hand, the fact that the costs are distributed unevenly. As emphasized by Elinor Ostrom,

An enforceable agreement among the major emitters of GHGs [greenhouse gases] will take a long time to develop. Given the lack of an enforceable international agreement to reduce GHG emissions, just waiting and doing nothing can defeat the possibilities of substantial remedy in time to prevent a major disaster. In addition to the problem of waiting too long, "global solutions" negotiated at a global level, if not backed up by a variety of efforts at national, regional, and local levels, are not guaranteed to work well. While the level of $CO_2$ and other GHGs in the atmosphere may be relatively uniformly distributed at a megascale, the impacts of climate change differentially affect localities and regions by their geographic location, ecological and economic conditions, prior preparation for extreme events, and past investments. (Elinor Ostrom 2010b)

At first this may seem like an insoluble problem, but her main point about this issue was to build upon an analogy to the earlier metropolitan debate. In her view, most people thinking about global environmental problems today are making the exact same error that the consolidationists have made in the 1960s, namely imagining that because the problem is global it requires a global administrative and regulatory body. The alternative is to think of ways of organizing the incentive structures at lower levels that would generate the desired global public good as an *emergent* outcome. In Elinor Ostrom's words,

The initial relevance of the polycentric approach [to the problem of global environmental problems] is the parallel between the earlier theoretical presumption that *only* the largest scale was relevant for the provision and production of public goods for metropolitan areas, and the contemporary presumption by some scholars that only the global scale is relevant for policies related to global public goods. Extensive empirical research found, however, that while large-scale units were part of effective governance of metropolitan areas, small- and medium-scale units were also necessary components. An important lesson is that simply recommending a single governance unit to solve global collective-action problems—because of global impacts—needs to be seriously rethought. (Elinor Ostrom 2010b)

More specifically, she points out that a *variety* of initiatives designed to lower GHGs emissions exist at the level of regions (e.g., the European Union), states, cities, and individuals. The standard perspective holds that any initiative is to be evaluated under the assumption that it would be adopted globally: "many analysts have presumed that an enforceable global agreement is the *only* way to address the threat of climate change" (Elinor Ostrom 2010b). But this is not likely to happen because of the transaction costs involved. However, a variety of initiatives happening at the same time may end up having the desired global effect in the aggregate, while each of them is easier to adopt at its own smaller scale (Cole 2015). In other words, initiatives adapted to the local conditions can all be pieces of a large global puzzle, although there is no single global puzzle solver:

> Given the complexity and changing nature of the problems involved in coping with climate change, "optimal" solutions for making substantial reductions in the level of GHGs emitted into the atmosphere are only a dream. A major reduction in emissions is, however, needed. The advantage of a polycentric approach is that it encourages experimentation by multiple actors, as well as the development of methods for assessing the benefits and costs of particular strategies adopted in one setting and comparing these with results obtained in other settings.... We need to recognize that doing nothing until a global treaty is negotiated maximizes the risk involved for everyone. Rather than only a global effort, it would be better to self-consciously adopt a polycentric approach to the problem of climate change in order to gain benefits at multiple scales as well as to encourage experimentation and learning from diverse policies adopted at multiple scales. (Elinor Ostrom 2010b)

## Entrepreneurship, Creative Destruction, and the Red Queen Race

The above discussion puts the problem of resilience outside the realm of simple textbook economics, which only deals with equilibrium

models. Before we see the Bloomington approach to public entrepreneurship (next chapter), it is useful to give a brief account of the
entrepreneurial approach to out-of-equilibrium processes. The first
hints about how to build an out-of-equilibrium theory were due to
Friedrich Hayek (1937). He noted that, before we assume that an
economy is in equilibrium, we should have a theory about the process
by which equilibrium would come about. He defined "equilibrium"
in the most general sense as a situation in which everyone's plans are
in harmony. This idea of equilibrium was later formalized in game
theory by the concept of Nash equilibrium—a situation in which no
one has the incentive to change their behavior. The idea was also further illustrated by Mises (1949, chap. 14, section 5), who coined the
term "evenly rotating economy." An evenly rotating economy is in
a steady-state equilibrium: exchange and production processes continue, but all relative prices remain unchanged; the equilibrium is not
static, but all the *flows* are constant and the probabilities of all events
remain unchanged.

The concept of the evenly rotating economy is useful for understanding the fundamental predicament of modern economies. As pointed out
by George Reisman (1996, 67–71), an evenly rotating economy can
only exist as long as *all* its resources are renewable. If one resource
is nonrenewable, as it gradually becomes depleted, its relative price
rises—hence, the economy is no longer in the steady-state equilibrium. The only way in which such economies continue is by a constant
process of discovering new production methods and substitutes. For
example, the only reason why we still have oil today is because of the
constant discovery of new oil extraction methods. If we still used the
oil extraction methods of the 1970s, oil would have already run out. In
other words, in an economy like ours, if technological progress slows
down too much, collapse follows. We cannot simply continue indefinitely with our current level of technology; to prevent collapse, we need
to constantly invent new things. This is similar to the Red Queen situation from *Alice in Wonderland*, when one needs to constantly run just to
keep in the same place. We can refer to this predicament as "Red Queen
growth," and define it by the condition that the rate of technological
improvement is greater or equal than the rate of resource depletion.
Importantly, Red Queen growth is not a steady-state equilibrium—not
even the flows remain constant. To use Schumpeter's expression, a constant process of "creative destruction," in which old methods are swept

away by new ones, is necessary for a complex society to survive (see Aligica and Tarko 2014a, chap. 4 for more). The only human societies that have been (approximately) evenly rotating economies are the hunter-gatherer societies. Up until ten thousand years ago when agriculture first emerged in the Fertile Crescent, for almost two hundred thousand years of Homo Sapiens's existence, these societies were able to maintain an unchanged way of life because they encompassed very few people (usually less than a hundred) and roamed across large-enough areas and whatever resources they were using could regenerate in time . By contrast, because of their larger populations, all agricultural societies have faced the Red Queen growth problem of nonrenewable resources, and most examples of dramatic societal collapses have involved their incapacity to find substitutes or improve production fast enough (Tainter 1988; Diamond 2005).

But the key lesson from these past societies is that collapse is ultimately a consequence of *institutional* failures. The reason why some societies fail and stumble at their Red Queen race is that their institutions fail to provide the proper incentives to further technological development. As Matt Ridley (2010, 30) put it, "[m]ost past bursts of human prosperity have come to naught because they allocated too little money to innovation and too much to asset price inflation or to war, corruption, luxury and theft." Economist William Baumol (1996) has famously framed the same idea in terms of how entrepreneurship is allocated in a society:

> If entrepreneurs are defined, simply, to be persons who are ingenious and creative in finding ways that add to their own wealth, power, and prestige, then it is to be expected that not all of them will be overly concerned with whether an activity that achieves these goals adds much or little to the social product or, for that matter, even whether it is an actual impediment to production. ... [T]he exercise of entrepreneurship can sometimes be unproductive or even destructive, and ... whether it takes one of these directions or one that is more benign depends heavily on the structure of payoffs in the economy—the rules of the game.

The Bloomington School account of institutions fits into this broader perspective focused on both knowledge and the incentives created by institutions. One simple approach to institutions is an equilibrium approach, according to which institutions are simply the equilibrium strategies emerging out of repeated interactions (Crawford and Ostrom

1995). But most social situations are too complicated to assume that such equilibrium has already been achieved. Consequently, one needs to focus instead on the processes of institutional change. As such, all complex social situations are a constant balancing act between, on one hand, monitoring and enforcement, and, on the other hand, opportunistic behavior and free-riding. Importantly, institutions can and are always being changed in response to (1) endogenous factors such as actors' opportunistic behavior, and (2) exogenous factors such as unexpected shocks.

To complement the focus on incentives, Hayek's (1937) key idea was that, to understand both the market process and the process of institutional change, one also needs to understand how knowledge is created and how it spreads. The reason why hunter-gatherers remained as evenly rotating economies for so long was that knowledge accumulated very slowly. The reason why so many past civilizations collapsed was that their institutional systems failed to spur fast enough growth of knowledge, and, hence, they lost their Red Queen race. And the reason why, so far, capitalist systems have experienced such an unprecedented boom since the Industrial Revolution is because of a combination of formal and informal institutions that spurred a tremendous increase in knowledge (Mokyr 1990). In his most famous article, "The use of knowledge in society" (1945), Hayek argued forcefully that, to understand complex societies, one needs to understand how local knowledge is produced and aggregated into a form (such as market prices) that can guide and coordinate large-scale human activities.

In the next chapter we will see in more detail the Institutional Analysis and Development (IAD) framework, which is key for thinking about institutional change. But what matters for now is to emphasize the idea that complex societies relying on nonrenewable resources cannot continue to exist and prosper unless they continuously innovate. And to do so, they need to make use of dispersed knowledge and provide incentives to innovation such that entrepreneurs use their talents in productive, rather than unproductive directions. This is connected to polycentricity, as

> [p]articipants in a polycentric system have the advantage of using local knowledge and learning from others who are also engaged in trial-and-error learning processes.... Polycentric systems tend to enhance innovation, learning, adaptation, trustworthiness, levels of cooperation

of participants, and the achievement of more effective, equitable, and sustainable outcomes at multiple scales, even though no institutional arrangement can totally eliminate opportunism with respect to the provision and production of collective goods. (Elinor Ostrom 2010b).

Polycentricity also has the advantage of making use of larger scale organizations when they are absolutely needed, in order to solve "problems associated with non-contributors, local tyrants, and inappropriate discrimination," as well as for making "major investments … in new scientific information and innovations" (Elinor Ostrom 2010b). As Elinor Ostrom often emphasized, "[n]o governance system is perfect, but polycentric systems have considerable advantages given their mechanisms for mutual monitoring, learning, and adaptation of better strategies over time" (Elinor Ostrom 2010b).

A polycentric system operates under certain overarching rules that the participants themselves create, monitor, and enforce. But what is the nature of those overarching rules such that the system is indeed resilient? To put it differently, what did societies like the Easter Island miss? As we'll see below, Elinor Ostrom's "design principles" aim to offer some clues about this important question. But the general, broad idea, stemming from the need to constantly overcome the Red Queen race, is that resilient systems are based on rules under which

- individuals personally benefit from cooperative and productive behavior, and are punished for free-riding and for unproductive or destructive behaviors, and
- individuals personally benefit from discovering new, improved methods for solving problems, and, along the idea of "creative destruction," they are free to pursue such avenues even if they are causing disruptions to established interests.

In other words, good institutions incentivize prosocial behavior and create the conditions for increasing knowledge.

## Summary

To summarize, a polycentric system tends to be more resilient than a monocentric one because it fares better on all the components of resilience (Table 4.1).

**Table 4.1.   Why Polycentric Systems Tend to Be More Resilient**

| Aspect of Resilience | Monocentric | Polycentric |
|---|---|---|
| Absorption capacity | *Lower*: Errors affect the entire system. Higher information costs lead to discovering the problem with a delay. | *Higher*: Errors only affect a subset of the system, and help is available from the other parts. Decision-makers that spot a problem can act on it immediately, before the problem becomes too large. |
| Speed of recovery | *Lower*: Information costs are higher, errors of "one-size-fits-all" solutions have wide-ranging effects. | *Higher*: Lower information costs, diversity of approaches facilitates learning. |
| Overoptimization | *More likely*: No inherent break on overoptimization until it's too late. Higher regulatory complexity. | *Less likely*: Decision-centers that overoptimize suffer costs long before the problem has the chance to expand to everybody. Simpler regulatory rules. |
| Slippery slopes | *More likely*: The cost of turning back from the current path is high. | *Less likely*: Individual decision-centers can unilaterally decide to change course, possibly saving the entire system. |
| Creative destruction | *Less*: Opportunities for substantial entrepreneurship exist mainly at the top. | *More*: Numerous opportunities for entrepreneurship at different levels. |

Polycentric systems tend to have higher absorption capacities because shocks do not affect simultaneously the whole system in the same way. Because they preserve institutional diversity, and hence epistemic diversity, they are less vulnerable to the problem of putting all their eggs in one basket. Similarly, apart from cases in which agreement on one common action is vital,[2] the speed of recovery tends to be higher in polycentric systems. Such systems are more market-like, and the information about who needs what has to travel a shorter chain of command. Furthermore, a diversity of approaches is available, which overcomes the problem of not knowing exactly which is the best solution and risking to place one's bet on the wrong solution. As discussed above, polycentric systems are much less vulnerable to the problem of overoptimization—of highly optimizing the whole system to previous challenges, opening up new vulnerabilities. The problem of slippery slopes is the most difficult to analyze objectively. Nonetheless, generally speaking, we can see that polycentric systems are less likely to fall prey to this problem simply because the cost of changing course is smaller. Finally, polycentric systems are far more entrepreneurial than monocentric ones because they allow a diversity of points of view to coexist, and not just in theory, but in practice.

## ELINOR OSTROM'S "DESIGN PRINCIPLES" FOR RESILIENT SYSTEMS

The above discussion explains why departures from the ideal of self-governance tend to create vulnerabilities. As Ridley (1996, 233) summarized it: "all sorts of commons problems are readily and frequently managed in sensible, virtuous, sustainable ways by local people who entirely lack the pretensions to be trained economists. Conversely, it becomes obvious that it is the very trained experts who often undo, destroy and wreck sensible arrangements for managing commons." But, as the Easter Island example suggests, this is not the end of the story. Self-governing solutions don't always work. So, the question is, what further conditions do polycentric systems need to satisfy?

[T]he core empirical and theoretical question is why self-organization is successfully undertaken in some cases and not in others. With better knowledge about what enhances local self-governance, it is possible to design larger-scale institutional arrangements that generate accurate information, provide open and fair conflict-resolution mechanisms, share risk, and back up efforts at local and regional levels. (Elinor Ostrom, interviewed by Aligica 2003)

Building on an "extraordinarily rich case-study literature...written by field researchers who had invested years of effort in obtaining detailed information about the strategies adopted by the appropriators of CPRs

**Table 4.2. Examples of Successful and Unsuccessful CPR Management**

| Location | Clear Boundaries | Congruence to Local Conditions | Inclusion | Monitoring | Graduated Sanctions | Conflict Resolution | Rights to Self-Organize | Nested Units | Institutional Performance |
|---|---|---|---|---|---|---|---|---|---|
| Torbel, Switzerland | Yes | Yes | Yes | Yes | Yes | Yes | Yes | — | Robust |
| Japanese mountain villages | Yes | Yes | Yes | Yes | Yes | Yes | Yes | — | Robust |
| Valencia, Murcia, and Oriheula, Spain | Yes | Yes | Yes | Yes | Yes | Yes | Yes | Yes | Robust |
| Raymond, West, and Central basins (now) | Yes | Yes | Yes | Yes | Yes | Yes | Yes | Yes | Robust |
| Alicante, Spain | Yes | Yes | Yes | Yes | Yes | Yes | Yes | Yes | Robust |
| Bacarra-Vintar, Philippines | Yes | Yes | Yes | Yes | Yes | Yes | Yes | Yes | Robust |
| Alanya, Turkey | NO | Yes | Weak | Yes | Yes | Weak | Weak | — | Fragile |
| Gal Oya, Sri Lanka | Yes | Yes | Yes | Yes | — | Weak | Weak | Yes | Fragile |
| Port Lameron, Canada | Yes | Yes | Weak | Yes | Yes | Yes | NO | NO | Fragile |
| Bay of Izmir and Bodrum, Turkey | NO | NO | NO | NO | NO | NO | Weak | NO | FAILURE |
| Mawelle, Sri Lanka | NO | yes | NO | Yes | Yes | NO | NO | NO | FAILURE |
| Kirindi Oya, Sri Lanka | yes | NO | NO | NO | NO | NO | NO | NO | FAILURE |
| Raymond, West, and Central basins (earlier) | NO | NO | NO | NO | NO | Yes | Yes | NO | FAILURE |
| Mojave groundwater basins | NO | NO | yes | NO | NO | Yes | Yes | NO | FAILURE |

*Source:* E. Ostrom 1990, 180, table 5.2.

[common-pool resources] and the rules they used" (Elinor Ostrom 1990, xv), she and her colleagues were able to create a list of "design principles." These principles are *general* and *broad* criteria regarding the institutional features that tend to favor resilience, but, as Elinor Ostrom has strongly emphasized, they do not provide very specific guidance. As the specific nature of the challenge differs from case to case, what works in one place may be counterproductive in another. And yet, successful systems manage to set up the same *types* of institutions, that is, specific institutions, which differ from case to case, which, nonetheless, fulfill the same set of important functions.

Ideally, these "design principles" would provide a list of necessary conditions for resilience, but, when she published *Governing the Commons*, she thought that we may still be a long way from fully establishing this (Elinor Ostrom 1990, 90–91). The work over the next 25 years since the publication of *Governing the Commons* has reinforced the value of these principles (Elinor Ostrom 2005a, chap. 9, 2010a; Cox, Arnold, and Villamayor Tomás 2010; Wilson, Ostrom, and Cox 2013).[3]

Table 4.2 showcases a short list of paradigmatic cases studies and how they fare against the list of "design principles" (based on Elinor Ostrom 1990, 180, table 5.2).[4] These principles describe "an essential element or condition that helps to account for the success of these institutions in sustaining the CPRs and gaining the compliance of generation after generation of appropriators to the rules in use" (Elinor Ostrom 1990, 90). We can see some of these principles as applying to the *operational level*, that is, they concern the actual operation of the activity (using irrigation when cultivating rice, fishing in the ocean, cutting wood from a forest, taking water from a groundwater basin, etc.). Other principles apply to the *collective choice level*, meaning they concern the methods by which the operational level rules are created, monitored, and enforced. And finally, the *constitutional level* principles specify the collective choice arenas and the rights to create new collective choice arenas.

## The Operational Level

In order for the resource to not be depleted or mismanaged, the following conditions must hold:

1. *Excludability principle*: Clearly defined group boundaries and membership

2. *Local fit principle*: Correspondence of appropriation rules to local conditions
3. *Fairness principle*: Proportionality between the benefits and costs of various actors
4. *Graduated sanctions principle*: Graduated sanctions for breaking the rules.

One way to understand them is to look at examples of CPRs that have been mismanaged as a result of failing to implement them:

1. The first principle is in many ways the most basic one. The source of the problem of CPRs is that, unlike the case of private goods, individuals cannot exclude others just by themselves (Table 3.1). As a result, CPRs end up as tragedy of the commons unless *the group* manages to create effective exclusion rules. If they do, the CPR is transformed into a club good, which is much easier to manage.[5]

A typical example of this problem is the Turkish fishing village, Bodrum, in the Aegean Sea. Up until the 1970s this was a successful fishing village, but then "the government of Turkey had encouraged some Bodrum fishers to construct larger trawling vessels" leading to a fleet of "100 small boats ... 11 trawlers, 2 purse seiners, and 9 bottom seiners, operated by approximately 400 fisheries" (Elinor Ostrom 1990, 144). The main problem was that villagers could not exclude outsiders from entering their waters and fishing there. The responsibility for doing so belonged to the Turkish government, which, however, "had rarely enforced the three-mile limit, much to the anger of the small fishermen" (Fikret Berkes, cited by Elinor Ostrom 1990, 144), and "the agency responsible for fishery rules (the Ministry of Agriculture) employed no agents to enforce those rules" (Elinor Ostrom 1990, 146).

2. The congruence of the rules to the local conditions is a more subtle idea, and it highlights the idea that institutions created in one environment cannot always be easily transplanted to another environment. This is one of the main reasons why, throughout her entire career, Elinor Ostrom has warned against "panaceas" and "blueprint thinking." In a sense, the original Hardin (1968) article that laid out the tragedy of the commons idea was a typical example of blueprint thinking, and of failing to understand the congruence principle. Because the underlining economic cause of tragedy of the commons is the same in all examples no matter how different, Hardin assumed that the solution would also

be the same—either privatizing the resource or centralized government control. Consider the following simple comparison to see why this is not true.

One way of solving a deforestation tragedy of the commons in a forest, due to people cutting down too many trees out of the commonly owned forest, is to parcel the forest and privatize each parcel. This way, each parcel is transformed into a private good, and it usually more likely to be properly managed. By contrast, this kind of solution is impossible for preventing overfishing in the ocean. One cannot parcel the ocean and privatize each parcel, simply because the fish move around. The privatization solution that can work in the case of the forest would fail in the case of the ocean fish. This is a simple example to highlight the point of the congruence principle. But in many cases, the congruence principle is much harder to apply because of considerable knowledge problems.

A particularly stark example of this is provided by the misguided attempt to reform the irrigation system in Bali and increase rice production (Lansing 1991). As Boettke (1996, 259) put it, this is an example when "the embodied wisdom in tradition exceeded the scientific *know how* of Western experts." The following happened:

> In the 1960s and early 1970s the International Rice Research Institute sought to eradicate the backward native practices of rice production throughout Asia... In Bali, the government introduced an agricultural policy in conformity with the "Green Revolution," which promoted continuous cropping of the new rice. Rice farmers were encouraged to plant rice without taking account of traditional irrigation schedules. The immediate effect, as could be expected, was a boost in rice production, but the policy soon resulted in a shortage of water and a severe outbreak of rice pests and diseases. (Boettke 1996, 259)

In this case, the problem was not so much one of bad incentives, but one created by the inherent complexity of the system, which made it difficult to predict what would happen when changes were introduced—the reforms broke the congruence principle *inadvertently*. The good intentions did not translate into good outcomes. As Boettke put it, the "customary practice was rooted in an understanding of the world which the enacted change failed to respect, and the result was an unintended undesirable outcome of good intentions in public policy" (Boettke 1996, 259–60).

3. The principle of fairness provides a key guide for creating a working incentive structure. While people might not be entirely selfish—for instance, they are often willing to enforce norms even at a personal cost (Fehr and Gächter 2002; Gintis et al. 2003)—they are not willing to let themselves exploited. The idea of fairness, understood as making benefits proportional to the effort that each person puts into the activity, is a general heuristic that people use in order to protect themselves against exploitation. Well-meaning top-down concerns often underestimate the extent of hard feelings that a perception of unfairness can generate.

For example, the irrigation problems in Gal Oya, Sri Lanka, have persisted and have led to an increasingly tense and distrustful relationship between farmers and the government because the government had not paid proper attention to the issue of fairness (or perceived fairness):

> The major weakness of the Gal Oya organization program was that farmers were expected to undertake construction [of the irrigation system] at the field-channel level without pay.... It probably was an unrealistic hope on the part of the planners to expect farmers to do hard physical work, with little immediate payoff, based simply on a nascent community spirit at the same time that private contractors were making substantial, often lucrative, profits for undertaking the same type of work. (Elinor Ostrom 1990, 171)

In the next chapter we will see how this failing irrigation system was eventually improved apparently against all odds. The point holds generally, although the exact practical application differs from case to case:

> In long-surviving irrigation systems, for example, subtly different rules are used in each system for assessing water fees used to pay for maintenance activities, but water tends to be allocated proportional to fees or other required inputs.... Sometimes water and responsibilities for resource inputs are distributed on a share basis, sometimes on the order in which water is taken, and sometimes strictly on the amount of land irrigated. No single set of rules defined for all irrigation systems in a region could satisfy the particular problems in managing each of these broadly similar, but distinctly different, systems. (Elinor Ostrom 2005a, 263)

4. The principle of graduated sanctions is a key common law concept, which, unsurprisingly, proves important for building resilient systems. The typical example given in law and economics textbooks is the following. Given that harsher punishments work better for deterring

behavior, why not use the harshest penalty for all offenses? Apart from various considerations of justice, a practical reason exists. Suppose, for instance, that house burglary would be punished as harshly as murder. This would create a greater incentive for burglars to kill the owners of the house, in cases when they would be caught in the act. For instance, if the act of burglary was punished by, say, twenty years in prison, the burglar may think that that is already so bad that anything that might help him escape is worth doing.

In case of CPR, penalties are required for preventing free-riding. Graduated sanctions have the role to distinguish among honest errors, neglect, and intentional wrongdoing:

> Graduated sanctions progress incrementally based on either the severity or the repetition of violations. Graduated sanctions help to maintain community cohesion while genuinely punishing severe cases; they also maintain proportionality between the severity of violations and sanctions, similar to the proportionality between appropriation and provision rules .... (Cox, Arnold, and Villamayor Tomás 2010)

What the above law and economics logic shows is that failures can occur not only when penalties are missing, but also if they are too harsh or do not properly distinguish between types of offenses.

## The Collective Choice Level

The details of the rules needed for managing a resource are often very complex, but the bottom line is that successful systems have good collective choice mechanisms—that is, good rules for making rules. What is a good collective choice arrangement? It is a system within which those who create the operational level rules have a strong vested interest of building a long-term productive system, which includes the concern for setting up effective mechanisms for monitoring and enforcing the rules. The three design principles that speak to these concerns are the following:

1. *Accountability principle*: Monitors and enforcers of rules are accountable for their actions.
2. *Political representation principle*: Most individuals affected by the rules are included in the collective choice group that can modify these rules.

3. *Conflict resolution principle*: Access to low-cost local arenas for conflict resolution providing decisions perceived as fair.

1. The principle of accountability is essential for building a trusting relationship between the community at large and those with positions of authority—be they external governmental officials or prominent members of the community. But, at first glance, the problem of effective monitoring may seem impossible: Who monitors the monitors? And who monitors those who monitor the monitors, etc.? This puzzle shows that, ultimately, all working systems are based on at least some rules being self-enforcing, that is, those subjected to the rules have a vested interest in enforcing the rules. Self-governance is the most powerful method of creating self-enforcing rules. This works by creating a circle of rules rather than an ever-growing linear hierarchy (Aligica and Tarko 2013, 2014c). In a group of people who they themselves take turns at being monitors, the self-interest problem is diminished to manageable levels because the monitor will now have a vested interest in making sure that the rules are followed. This is further helped by the fact that, in many cases, "monitoring is a natural by-product of using the commons" (Elinor Ostrom 1990, 96).[6]

Even when the monitors are hired from outside the community, and the complexity of the system thus increases by involving more people, the monitors would still have the desire to uphold the rules in order to satisfy the demand of those who pay them. The major problems usually occur when monitors are appointed from outside the community. This makes the "who monitors the monitors" problem difficult because outsiders usually have less of a vested interest in the well-being of the community than the community itself, and, hence, often don't or can't monitor the monitors very well. It is then not surprising that "[m]ost long-surviving resource regimes select their own monitors, who are accountable to the appropriators or are appropriators themselves and who keep an eye on resource conditions as well as on harvesting activities" (Elinor Ostrom 2005a, 295). The system usually works along the following lines:

> The community creates an official position. In some systems appropriators rotate in this position so everyone has a duty to be a monitor. In other systems, all participants contribute resources and they jointly hire monitors. With local monitors, conditional operators are assured that someone

is generally checking on the conformance of others to local rules. Thus, they can continue their own cooperation without constant fear that others are taking advantage of them. (Elinor Ostrom 2005a, 295)

We have already seen the importance of this concern in Chapter 1, in the case of community policing. The issue of trust, making sure that the monitors and enforcers can be relied upon to act without discriminating against some members while favoring others, is essential for building successful communities. It is for this reason that "[m]onitors may not perform satisfactorily if they do not directly benefit from improved resource conditions. Thus, it may be important that monitors are accountable to those who most depend on the resource." (Cox, Arnold, and Villamayor Tomás 2010). As an example, consider the case of two forests in the Middle Hills of Nepal. Researchers

found that the ability of local users to oversee monitors' performance affected resource conditions. In Jylachitti Forest, local users hired two people for regular monitoring and paid them through contributions from each member household. In Dhulkhel Forest, guards were also hired, but they were paid by local authorities. Whereas Jylachitti local users were engaged in supervising the guards' performance in controlling timber extraction levels, this was not the case in Dhulkhel, where overextraction was becoming an issue by the end of the study. (Cox, Arnold, and Villamayor Tomás 2010)

The problem of accountability in monitoring and enforcing rules is also closely connected to the issue of corruption. One reason many systems fail is not because of ignorance, but because the failure actually benefits a small subset of people. For example, Elinor Ostrom cites Robert Bates's *Essays on the Political Economy of Rural Africa* to point out that major "inefficiencies persist because they are politically useful; economic inefficiencies afford governments means of retaining political power" (Robert Bates, cited by Elinor Ostrom 2005a, 277). In the economic literature, this kind of inefficiency is described as "rent seeking"—referring to the resources people use, not in productive activities, but in trying to obtain politically granted privileges (Buchanan, Tullock, and Tollison 1980; Baumol 1996; Aligica and Tarko 2014b). Such privileges cause economic inefficiencies themselves, but the biggest inefficiency is due to the fact that people divert resources from productive activities to privilege-seeking activities. As pointed out by Elinor Ostrom,

> The losses that the general consumer and taxpayer accrue from rent-seeking activities are one dimension. The second aspect of rent seeking in highly centralized economies is the acquisition of resources needed to accumulate and retain political power. All forms of opportunistic behavior, therefore, are exacerbated in an environment in which an abundance of funds is available for the construction of new and frequently large-scale infrastructure project that provide subsidized electricity, local roads, schools, and water. (Elinor Ostrom 2005a, 278)

The point about such infrastructure projects is not that they are not needed, but that the *method* by which they are created and the *reasons* for their creation make it unlikely that they are going to be properly designed, in particular that they are going to solve the monitoring problem. For example, "[m]illions of dollars have been poured into the development of irrigation works in the dry zone of Sri Lanka" (Elinor Ostrom 1990, 157), and yet the system failed for decades after decades.

2. Many attempts to manage common property involve the use of central governments. As we have seen above, this often makes it difficult to create a proper system of incentives with respect to monitoring and enforcement because the central government has less of a vested interest in the well-being of various communities than they themselves have, and it is vulnerable to rent-seeking. Beyond this "mere" problem of monitoring and enforcement lies the issue of creating the rules in the first place. The political representation principle states that rules are more likely to be efficient when they are created from the bottom-up, by the participation of those who are ultimately subjected to those rules. The members of the local community are both more likely to have the relevant knowledge about the details of the problems affecting them, and have a greater incentive to find effective solutions. The knowledge problem is even more significant when "environments change over time, [and] being able to craft local rules is particularly important as officials located far away do not know of the change" (Elinor Ostrom 2005a, 263).

For example, when researchers studied 48 different irrigation systems in India, they have found that "the quality of the maintenance of irrigation canals is significantly lower on those systems where farmers perceive the rules to have been made by a local elite" (Elinor Ostrom

2005a, 264). Similarly, "in all villages where a government agency decides how water is to be allocated and distributed, frequent rule violations are reported, and farmers tend to contribute less to the local village fund" (Elinor Ostrom 2005a, 264). The bottom line is that the political representation principle, while not guaranteeing that the community makes good rules, is necessary for the rules to be perceived as legitimate. As a result of greater legitimacy, voluntary rule compliance is more likely. Also, monitoring and enforcement is easier, especially when they involve a certain element of coproduction. I return to this issue in the next chapter.

3. Due to the nature of common-pool resources, a certain level of rivalry is inescapable. If someone takes too much water out of the irrigation system, less is available for others. If someone uses ultra-efficient fishing methods, like large trawlers or nets, or fishes during the spawning period, less fish is left for other fishermen. If someone cuts down too many trees from the communally owned forest, fewer trees are left for others.

Even when good rules are created to prevent the tragedy of the commons from occurring, and even when monitoring works well, conflicts are still bound to happen. The situation on the ground is always more complicated than whatever the rules can codify. A certain level of arbitrariness cannot be avoided. Because of this, it is essential that effective avenues for conflict resolution exist—institutions that can deliver a quick and fair solution to conflicts. Elinor Ostrom points out that dysfunctional systems often fail to provide effective conflict resolution. For example, in dysfunctional fishing villages in Turkey, fishers go as far as burning each other's nets, and in central Sri Lanka, violence between farmers competing for the same limited amount of irrigation water is not an unusual occurrence (Elinor Ostrom 1990, chap. 5).

Conflict resolution also has a more subtle aspect involving "discussing and resolving what constitutes an infraction" (Elinor Ostrom 1990, 100). This is necessary because "individuals who are seeking ways to slide past or subvert rules, there are always various ways in which they can 'interpret' a rule so that they can argue they have complied with the rule, but in effect subverting its intent" (Elinor Ostrom 1990, 100). For example,

Even such a simple rule as "each irrigator must send one individual for one day to help clean the irrigation canals before the rainy season begins" can be interpreted quite differently by different individuals.... Does sending a child below the age of 10 or an adult above age 70 to do heavy physical work meet this rule? Is working for four hours or six hours a "day" of work? Does cleaning the canal immediately next to one's own farm qualify for this community obligation? (Elinor Ostrom 1990, 100)

Successful communities thus manage to achieve consensus about what exactly amounts to performing one's obligations, and, for cases when conflict still occurs, create working arrangements that are perceived to provide fair outcomes in a timely fashion.

## The Constitutional Level

The above emphasis on self-governance leads us to "constitutional" considerations, meaning the rules about creating collective choice arenas. There are two important principles in this regard:

1. *Subsidiarity principle*: External governmental authorities recognize, at least to some extent, the right to self-organize.
2. *Polycentricity principle*: "Appropriation, provision, monitoring, enforcement, conflict resolution, and governance activities are organized in multiple layers of nested enterprises" (Elinor Ostrom 2005a, 259).

We have already seen why polycentricity is such an important concept, both from the point of view of efficiency (Chapters 1 and 2) and from the point of view of resilience (earlier in this chapter). Before ending this chapter, let me briefly address the subsidiarity principle.

The key point that the subsidiarity principle brings to the table is that, while self-governance often happens naturally, as people try to find ways to solve conflicts and build rules (Leeson 2014), it is also vulnerable to top-down disruptions. An intrusive central government may not just fail to establish the proper rules and effective monitoring mechanisms, but it may also disrupt, hamper, or prevent local attempts to solve the local problems.

For example, it is usually the case that

local fishers devise extensive rules defining who can use a fishing ground and what kind of equipment can be used. Provided the external government officials give at least minimal recognition to the legitimacy of such rules, the fishers themselves may be able to enforce the rules themselves. But if external government officials presume that only they have the authority to set the rules, then it will be very difficult for local appropriators to sustain a rule-governed CPR over the long run. (Elinor Ostrom 1990, 101)

This is because those who are subjected to the local rules, and who may want to "get around the rules created by the fishermen... may go to the external government and try to get local rules overturned" (Elinor Ostrom 1990, 101).

To highlight the importance of subsidiarity, and also how the central government may act as a catalyst for local self-governance, rather than as a disrupter, consider two examples of fisheries from the United States (Elinor Ostrom 1999, 2012).

The lobster fisheries in Maine were severely depleted in the 1920s, as local communities were failing in their attempts to effectively manage the fisheries. The state intervened by threatening some of the fisheries with closure, but, rather than setting up its own top-down comprehensive fishery policy, it merely "supported informal local enforcement efforts" (Elinor Ostrom 1999). The intervention was successful and "[b]y the late 1930s, compliance problems were largely resolved and stocks had rebounded" (Elinor Ostrom 1999). A more recent state intervention was to transform these informal local organizations, which were beginning to break down, into formalized councils with democratic local elections and formalized authority over specified geographical areas. This had an unexpected beneficial consequence, when "the formalization of local zones was followed, almost immediately, by the creation of an informal council of councils to address problems at a greater than-local scale" (Elinor Ostrom 1999). This highlights one of the main ideas that V. Ostrom, Tiebout, and Warren (1961) have emphasized: that cooperation between communities in regard to large-scale problems can often emerge from bottom-up.

Another interesting example is that of Washington state Pacific salmon fisheries. Prior to the mid-1970s, they were centrally managed and, as Elinor Ostrom notes, they faced a typical knowledge problem: the "centrally regulated system had focused on aggregations of species and spent little time on the freshwater habitats that are essential to maintain the viability of salmon fisheries over the long term" (E. Ostrom 1999).

In the mid-1970s, the management system changed due to a major court decision that granted to "Indian tribes that had signed treaties more than a century before" the right "to 50 percent of the fish that passed through the normal fishing areas of the tribes" (E. Ostrom 1999). Consequently, "[t]his has required the state to develop a 'co-management' system that involves both the state of Washington and the 21 Indian tribes in diverse policy roles related to salmon" (E. Ostrom 1999). The change drastically reshaped the system of incentives at the local level. On one hand, the state continued involvement assured the individual tribes that free-riding by other tribes wasn't going to be tolerated and, thus, that conservation efforts were worthwhile. On the other hand, the comanagement system gave individual tribes an important economic stake in the resource, which, in turn, stimulated them to solve the aforementioned knowledge problem.

## How General Are These Principles?

These "design principles" are not without their critics (see Cox, Arnold, and Villamayor Tomás 2010 for a good overview). The most important concern is that they are not exhaustive, that is, that some systems may still fail for *other* reasons, cultural or environmental, despite following all of Ostrom's principles.

To some extent, Vincent Ostrom's long-time concerns with how people develop and learn the "art of association" touches upon this (V. Ostrom 1991b, 1997). One way to interpret this is to argue that a *meta-constitutional* level exists, which covers culture (Elinor Ostrom and Ostrom 2004). Various cultural considerations may provide legitimacy to some rules but not to others (Boettke 1996). Also, in different cultural environments, different institutional solutions for the same kind of problem may be developed—what Lavoi and Chamlee-Wright (2001) call "cultural comparative advantage." This also explains why institutional reforms proposed from the outside often fail to "stick"—when they are incongruous with the local cultural milieu, the institutional reforms proposed by outsiders are seen as illegitimate in various ways by locals, which leads to all the compliance and monitoring problems discussed earlier (Boettke, Coyne, and Leeson 2008). Table 4.3 summarizes this idea.

Table 4.3.  Institutional Stickiness: The Likelihood that a Reform Will Persist

|  |  | Reform Is Introduced at the Initiative of | |
|---|---|---|---|
|  |  | *Locals* | *External decision-makers* |
| **Origin of the idea** | *Local* | Very high stickiness | Low stickiness |
|  | *External* | High stickiness | Very low stickiness |

As far as the idea that we should also include certain environmental considerations among the principles, this objection actually misses the point entirely (Aligica and Tarko 2014c). A simple way to see why is to think of the Haiti–Chile comparison with which I've started this chapter. We can also think of other similar comparisons. For example, why is it that the Netherlands is less endangered by the rise of sea level than Bangladesh? A large part of Netherlands is already under sea level, and yet it is in no immediate danger. What such comparisons point out is that it is not the environmental challenge per se that matters—it is whether the institutional system in place has a high capacity to cope with challenges. Gradual sea rises threaten Netherlands less endangered than Bangladesh simply because Netherlands is richer and can afford to invest massive sums of money in technological solutions such as dikes. A similar explanation holds for the Haiti–Chile comparison. Figures 4.2 and 4.3 also showcase the impact of different institutions upon environmental protection, by looking at the same resource on two sides of a border. In the Haiti–Dominican Republic comparison, different institutions have led to complete deforestation in one case versus a sustainable forest in the other. In the Germany–Czech Republic comparison, we see how, on one side, the bark beetle has been successfully contained, while on the other side, it has devastated the forest.

The institutional approach proposed by Elinor Ostrom is not thus *ignoring* environmental factors, it is instead trying to go deeper. The proximate cause of catastrophes is obviously some shock, such as an earthquake. This is not the mystery. The mystery that needs clearing

Figure 4.2.   The Border between Haiti and Dominican Republic. (*Source*: United Nations Environment Programme.)

Figure 4.3.   The Border between Germany and Czech Republic. (*Source*: Bavarian Forest Sumava National Park.)

up is why some places are much better able to cope with greater shocks than others. And for this we need the institutional approach. Another important question is whether this synthesis of relatively small-scale systems applies to larger scale systems. Cox, Arnold, and Villamayor Tomás (2010) argue that

> it seems plausible that several of the principles would be applicable to higher levels of governance.... Proportionality of costs and benefits, conflict-resolution mechanisms, nested institutional arrangements, and effective and participatory collective-choice arrangements seem particularly relevant. The applicability of the design principles to a higher level of governance is not a claim that communities can necessarily resolve large-scale environmental problems.

The nature and reason of these "design principles" is perhaps best clarified by an important theoretical article, in which Elinor Ostrom collaborated with well-known evolutionary biologist E. O. Wilson, and, Michael Cox, one of the main drivers behind the development of the social–economical systems (SES) framework for understanding large-scale systems. In this article, they argue that the "design principles" are not ad hoc, but they are a way in which social groups manage to cope with the fact that individuals have various cognitive limitations . As such, there are good reasons to believe that the relevance of these principles goes far beyond the initial set of empirical cases that Elinor Ostrom and her colleagues have analyzed, but ultimately this is an empirical matter which requires more study.

## NOTES

1. The U.S. Geological Survey estimates 100,000, while a study by the University of Michigan estimates 160,000 (Kolbe et al. 2010).
2. In such cases, decision-making costs in the polycentric system can render it too costly to make adequate decisions quickly.
3. The main difference is with regard to Ostrom's Principle 2, which in the earlier studies refers to the congruence of governance rules to local conditions, while in the later works it also refers to fairness considerations (compare Elinor Ostrom 1990, 90, with 2005a, 259). Following Cox, Arnold, and Villamayor Tomás' (2010) suggestion, I include these two ideas separately, which is why my list has nine principles, rather than just eight.

4. She later complained about the label "design principles" as it suggests a top-down and constructivist approach, which is the very opposite of what she had in mind. The term "design principles" is fairly common in mathematical literature on resilience in complexity theory, which, as we have seen, has provided significant insight to Elinor Ostrom and her collaborators.

5. Cox, Arnold, and Villamayor Tomás (2010) point out that we should bear in mind two distinct kinds of boundaries: the boundaries of the resource and the membership of users to the group of legitimate users.

6. Cox, Arnold, and Villamayor Tomás (2010) note that monitoring users and monitoring the resource are sometimes different. For example, the resource might need monitoring because of varying environmental conditions that have nothing to do with human activities.

## Chapter Five

# Hamilton's Dilemma

## *Can Societies Establish Good Governments by Reflection and Choice?*

> The moment we utter the words "The State" a score of intellectual ghosts rise to obscure our vision. Without our intention and without our notice, the notion of "The State" draws us imperceptibly into a consideration of the logical relationship of various ideas to one another, and away from facts of human activity. It is better, if possible, to start from the latter and see if we are not led thereby into an idea of something which will turn out to implicate the marks and signs which characterize political behavior. (John Dewey, *The Public and Its Problems*, cited by V. Ostrom 1997, 40)

We are used to describing collective entities as if they are individuals. We talk about "firms" and "organizations" as having goals. We talk about "states" as having "national interests" and we describe international relations as relations between states. We even talk about "society" as if it's an individual—for instance, we are concerned about promoting "general welfare" and we may talk about "national character."

It may seem a tedious point to make, but, of course, none of these entities *really* have interests—only the individual people within these organizations *actually* have goals and beliefs. Is this just a pedantic and useless point? People like John Dewey and Vincent Ostrom clearly thought not. Elinor Ostrom's Nobel Prize address also focused on why we should look "beyond markets and states," in the sense of becoming more fully aware of the limitations of these concepts, and also of the conceptual possibilities beyond them. Vincent Ostrom stressed that "[m]yths and the misplaced use of abstractions to apply to Societies as

*Photo 6. Elinor and Vincent Ostrom at Confucius Temple, in Front of a Statue of
Confucius (2007). (Source: Digital Library of the Commons, Indiana University)*

a Whole need to be recognized for what they are—less than empirically
warrantable assertions" (V. Ostrom 1997, 60), and he complained that
"[t]he overwhelming amount of political discourse in the mass media,
among students and faculty on university campuses, and in casual discussions contains references to 'America,' 'Society,' 'the Nation,' and
'the Government'" (p. 70). He thought that "as intellectual constructs,
they are too gross to be useful; they run the risk of being misleading
and are the source of serious forms of deception and misconceptions"
(p. 111).

When someone brings the same point over and over every 20 pages or so, you can tell it really irks him. And when someone puts this in the very title of their Nobel Prize address, you may guess she thinks it's important. When people came to give various paper presentations at Bloomington, Vincent Ostrom would often derail them by insisting that they should rigorously define their concepts, sometimes thumping his fist on the table to give more weight to the argument. Peter Boettke tells the humorous story of how he was supposed to give a presentation about postcommunist transition and Vincent kept insisting that he needed to define more clearly what he meant by "The Market." Boettke now notes that Ostrom was actually making a very important point which, in the 1990s, was lost on most economists who argued about privatization: markets are underpinned by a complex set of institutions, defining and enforcing private property and contracts, and one cannot properly talk about privatization without talking about these institutions.

Vincent Ostrom was particularly concerned about the possibility that language may be used to hide important truths instead of revealing them:

> A language primarily devoted to the "form of Government," the "State," or "*power*" relationships" may focus human perceptions in ways that neglect what needs to be taken into account. ... If the language of the political sciences includes only a portion of what is constitutive of democratic societies, political scientists cannot understand how such societies work. They do not understand how the essential working parts relate to one another. What does it mean for people to govern? If our understanding is inadequate, our language is likely to be inappropriate. (V. Ostrom 1997, 34–35)

In other words, he feared that by focusing on overly aggregated concepts like "The State," "The Government," "The Nation," "Society," etc., we are actually missing the very important details about what makes democracies actually work. Throughout their work, the Bloomington School tried to reveal the private and civil society mechanisms that underpin self-governing communities and make democracies more resilient. Their concern in this regard can hardly be overstated:

> [O]ne of our greatest priorities at the Workshop has been to ensure that our research contributes to the education of future citizens, entrepreneurs in the public and private spheres, and officials at all levels of government. We have a distinct obligation to participate in this educational

process as well as to engage in the research enterprise so that we build a cumulative knowledge base that may be use to sustain democratic life. Self-governing, democratic systems are always fragile enterprises. Future citizens need to understand that they participate in the constitution and reconstitution of rule-governed polities. And they need to learn the "art and science of association." If we fail in this, all our investigations and theoretical efforts are useless. (Elinor Ostrom, interviewed by Aligica 2003)

Their basic claim was that

Democratic societies cannot be fashioned without such roots of self-governance.... For this reason, the basic architecture of modern societies must, as Tocqueville has argued, draw upon a science of association to fashion rules of social interaction that apply from the level of the village to the level of the nation state and beyond. (Vincent Ostrom, interviewed by Aligica 2003)

This being said, such claims, as well as the insistence on more precise language, still strikes most people as an exaggeration. Part of this reaction is purely pragmatic: First of all, speaking of collective entities *as if* they are units with goals and beliefs is a useful approximation which works for many purposes. *Of course* we know that, strictly speaking, only individual people really have intentions. Second, what alternative do we have? Decomposing these structures all the way to the individual level is tedious and unnecessarily complicated.

Building on Dennett (1989, 1995), I'm going to refer to this as the *intentional stance* to institutions and organizations, and also, less neutrally, as *institutional anthropomorphism*. The intentional stance is simply the pragmatic decision to try to describe and predict some behaviors of X by assigning goals and beliefs to X, regardless of whether X "really" has them. The intentional stance often works well, but, when it's abused, we usually refer to the problem of anthropomorphizing X. When Richard Feynman was talking about how electrons "want" to occupy the lowest energy level in an atom, we're thinking she's just being cute; but when your electrician starts to assign goals to the electric current in your house, you're starting to worry they might not be entirely competent. With this distinction in mind, Vincent and Elinor Ostrom's objections could be described as wagging their fingers at those who anthropomorphize society or the state.

The Bloomington School did not object to pragmatist justifications per se, and the Ostroms may have been pragmatists themselves . On one hand, as illustrated above, they thought that the simplicity of the anthropomorphic approximations also carries significant costs in terms of obscuring relevant truths. They objected on purely pragmatic grounds, rather than on some ontological grounds about how things "really are." For example, talking about international relations purely as relations between countries with different "national interests," and their expectations about one another, will obscure the importance of rent-seeking factors and the importance of domestic politics. But such factors might be highly relevant in a predictive sense. They lead us to form different expectations about how various international relations will turn out.

On the other hand, and this brings us to the main subject of this chapter, they *did* create an alternative framework of analysis. This framework is known as the Institutional Analysis and Development (IAD) framework (Elinor Ostrom and Ostrom 2004; Elinor Ostrom 2005a, 2011a, 2014; Hess and Ostrom 2006, chap. 3; McGinnis 2011; Oakerson and Parks 2011; Tarko in Elinor Ostrom 2012). In conjunction with the concept of "public entrepreneurship" (Elinor Ostrom 1965, 2005b; Oakerson and Parks 1988), it provides a very different account of how institutions work and how they change. This framework has proven quite successful. So successful in fact, that many practitioners, who use it on a daily basis to make sense of their particular problems of interest, are not exactly familiar with the deep philosophical stakes described above. What's at stake is to provide a method of zooming in and out of organizations and institutions, which is less vulnerable to misinterpretations and less likely to be misleading and a "source of serious forms of deception and misconceptions." Practitioners clearly find the IAD framework useful. But does this mean that everyone should switch to using it and abandon anthropomorphizing institutions and organizations?

This brings us to what Dennett (1989, chap. 2, 1991) has called the problem of "real patterns." How do we know when a legitimate use of the intentional stance veers into an unfortunate form of anthropomorphizing? He uses the following example. Suppose that people's behavior is fully determined by the activity of their brain. Does this mean that people don't "really" have intentions and beliefs? Dennett argues "no"—even if assigning intentions and beliefs to a person is, from the point of view of their brain activity, a highly aggregated enterprise, it nonetheless captures a "real pattern" of their behavior. The fact that their behavior *can* be relatively accurately predicted on the basis of intentions and beliefs means that this simplified model is, in a sense, true. Moreover, he points out that we identify "dysfunctions" on the basis of failures of the intentional stance. For instance, if someone has incoherent preferences or if they constantly choose means at odds with their stated goals, we don't say that the intentional stance has failed, we say that there's something wrong with that person (they are being "irrational" or they are lying about their goals).

The same kind of argument about "real patterns" applies more generally. For instance, unlike the Ostroms, Douglass North put a lot of weight on a notoriously vague distinction between organizations and institutions. I think we can understand this distinction based on the "real patterns" criterion. Organizations are institutional arrangements, that is, systems of rules, for which the intentional stance works well. For instance, strictly speaking, firms don't "really" have goals and beliefs—only their employees and shareholders have. We can, however, successfully use the intentional stance to describe and predict how firms behave. In fact, a "dysfunctional" firm or organization is precisely one that doesn't pursue its goals coherently and/or effectively. If that happens, we need to look more carefully at the interactions within the firm, but otherwise the intentional stance is usually good enough.

By contrast, institutions like the ones described in the previous chapters cannot be anthropomorphized. This is not a sign of dysfunction—but a sign of their complexity. As Douglass North intuited, their nature is very different from that of organizations. They are both institutions in the sense that they are systems of rules, but other than that they are very different. They may be made out of the same "material," but they work on very different principles. This of course is precisely Ostroms' point when they emphasize polycentricity and argue against hierarchical arrangements of public economies. Hierarchical arrangement may be perfectly fine for organizations, but far less so for complex institutions like the provision of police services in a metropolitan area or the governance of an irrigation system with many users.

We can, thus, reframe Ostroms' objections to the use of collective concepts like "The State," "The Market," "Society," etc. as saying that these are not organizations (in North's sense)—they are complex institutional arrangements that cannot be properly understood with the intentional stance. If we want to understand states or societies, we should not anthropomorphize them. We need some other conceptual framework. And, indeed, the IAD framework is here to provide that alternative.

How was the creation of this alternative framework possible? It should be no surprise by now that it was not the result of armchair philosophizing. It resulted from an effort to solve practical applications. As noted in previous chapters, when Elinor Ostrom and her collaborators first started to study the governance of common-pool resources (CPRs), they collected a staggering large number of case studies from across disciplines. Comparing them was a real challenge. From a practical point of view, the aim was to, first, create a framework for analysis that would allow researchers to describe different cases in a consistent manner, such that they could be compared, and, second, discover a set of heuristics describing the conditions that favor resilience and long-term sustainable development (Elinor Ostrom's "design principles" described in the previous chapter). The IAD framework was developed for the analysis of relatively small-scale systems (Elinor Ostrom 1990, 2005a; Elinor Ostrom, Gardner, and Walker 1994; McGinnis 2011), while the Social–Ecological Systems (SES) framework was later developed with large-scale systems in mind (Elinor Ostrom 2009; Elinor Ostrom and Cox 2010; Cox 2014).

Vincent Ostrom (interviewed by Aligica 2003) described their approach in the following way (emphasis added):

> We try to combine formal approaches, fieldwork and experiments in order to "penetrate" social reality rather than to use formal techniques to "distance" ourselves from it, as Walter Eucken once expressed the difference. *We seek to find a fit between the conceptual framework used by the researcher and the framework used and shared by the people we are trying to study.* The researcher or observer needs to take into account the way people think about and experience themselves and their situation.

The IAD framework is the attempt to describe the world in a way that keeps the participants inside the model.

## THE INSTITUTIONAL ANALYSIS AND DEVELOPMENT (IAD) FRAMEWORK

The key to developing the IAD framework was the search for a correct way to partition complex systems into simpler components. Costanza et al. (2000) build upon the issue of recognizing the multiscale nature of SES. This issue raises the challenge of how to set the proper scale of analysis: "If we are correct that large systems are not 'small system grown large,' [model building] is directly tied to the problem of aggregation.... In complex, non-linear, discontinuous systems—like ecological and economic systems—aggregation is a far-from-trivial problem" (p. 7). The challenge is, however, not insurmountable because "ecosystems appear to function as partitionable systems." This makes the analysis possible:

> If ecosystems actually functioned as a seamless web with no practical subdivisions, understanding and managing such systems would require a massive, centralized modeling, measurement, and monitoring effort. Any missing piece or assumption could render the model useless. On the other hand, if ecosystems can be partitioned into relatively separable parts that are largely understandable on their own, measurement and monitoring requirements might still be great, but the ability to partition the problem would make understanding and managing the overall system much more tractable. More importantly, the need to pass large amounts of information along to a centralized management structure could be reduced greatly with little loss of understanding and management capability. Finally, the variety and appropriateness of regulatory responses could be increased if each such subunit responded independently to local disturbances; this would enhance the overall responsiveness of the system. (p. 8)

The IAD framework opens the door for analyzing "nested action arenas." The robustness of an SES is to a very large extent the consequence of the *correct partitioning* of the overall system into quasi-independent subsystems. This partitioning should give sufficient control and independence to subsystems such that they can react quickly to new challenges (much more quickly than if they were required to get permission for their actions from a distant, central-management level), but, at the same time, should preserve a certain degree of aggregation such that various important social goals are not lost as each local subgroup pursues its own narrow goals.

The IAD framework can be used to describe the inner workings of various institutional entities and the key idea that interests us here is that it is the tool to be utilized to describe both institutional structure *and* institutional change. By extension, the IAD framework allows us to analyze the relationship between a social–institutional system and

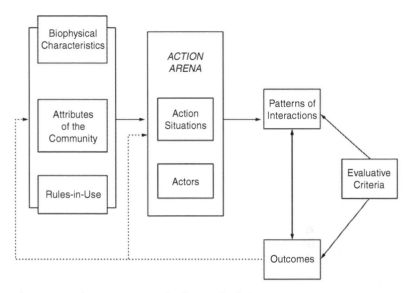

**Figure 5.1.   The IAD Framework: The Standard Figure.**

its natural environment (Elinor Ostrom, Gardner, and Walker 1994). In fact, the tool was forged during Ostrom's work on CPRs and their management.

The IAD framework has a reputation of being somewhat difficult to understand. Consider three alternative ways of representing it. Figure 5.1 gives a brief overview of the key conceptual elements, and it is the most commonly used figure in the literature. See Hess and E. Ostrom (2006, chap. 3) for a useful walkthrough of all the elements in the figure. Practitioners use this by specifying the biophysical characteristics of concern, the types of users ("attributes of the community"), and the rules-in-use at different levels (operational, collective choice, and constitutional). Figure 5.2 shows the same framework, but focused on better representing how "action situations" come into play by involving a subset of the possible participants and resources, as a result of some event. Finally, Figure 5.3 presents the framework once again, but with a focus on the rules involved and the process of evaluation and institutional redesign. Figure 5.3 illustrates the procession from (1) rules-in-use setting up (2) an action arena, which (3) generates patterns of interactions between participants and specific outcomes, which, in turn, are evaluated by the participants generating a feedback loop by

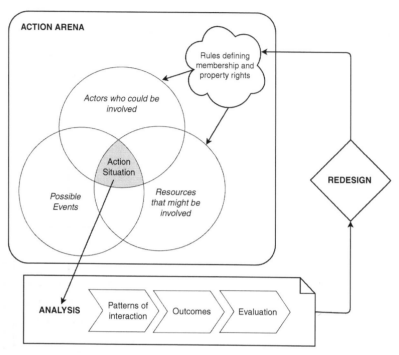

Figure 5.2.   **The IAD Framework: How Action Situations Form.**

(4) creating the incentive for some participants to try to redesign some of the rules.

## Action Arenas and Institutional Roles

The "action arena" is the replacement of institutional anthropomorphism. Instead of thinking of complex institutions as if they were unified agents with goals and beliefs, we describe them as action arenas that generate outcomes. An action arena is defined by its rules which specify membership and property rights, along the lines described earlier in Chapters 3 and 4. We can see an action arena as the set of all potential "action situations"—concrete situations in which a subset of the actors react to some events with respect to some of their resources of interest. At any time, there are other actors in the action arena who are not involved in the current action situation, and there are other resources, potentially of interest, but which are not the object of the

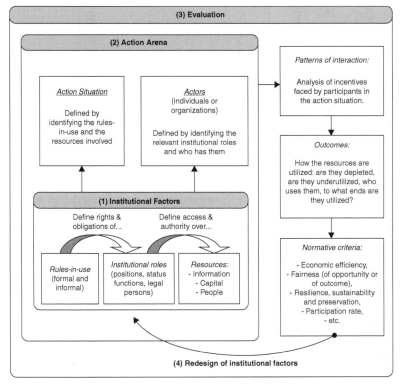

**Figure 5.3. The IAD Framework: Unpacking the Institutional Development Process.**

current situation. The Venn diagram in the action arena in Figure 5.2 is meant to illustrate this. You should think of the intersection of {the set of all actors} with {the set of all possible events} and {the set of all resources} as changing in time—hence generating a series of different action situations. We can also think of several different action situations occurring simultaneously. The patterns of interactions differ from action situation to action situation, but, because all action situations in a given action arena are underpinned by the same rules, we're interested in an aggregated picture of these patterns over many situations. The outcomes are the result of the accumulation of the results of many action situations over time.

The actors should be understood as people occupying certain institutional roles or positions. For example, institutional roles important

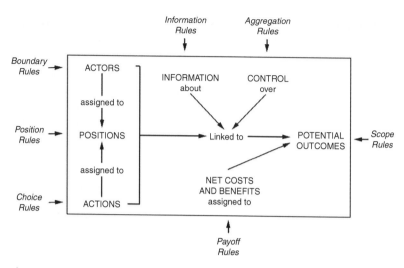

**Figure 5.4. The IAD Framework: Inside an Action Situation. (*Source:* Elinor Ostrom, various publications)**

for the issue of socioecological resilience are *users* and *providers* of a resource, and *policy-makers* who draft rules about access and usage of the resource (see Table 3.2 again for the more general approach). The bundle of rights and obligations that defines a particular institutional role defines access to *information* and *capital* (resources), and *authority* over other people with different institutional roles. Property rights are one of the most important components of an institutional role, and as we have seen in Chapter 3, they have been described as a bundle of rights.

In the most general account, we can zoom in on the action situation to find the details described in Figure 5.4 (Elinor Ostrom 2005a, 189, 2010a). Each of the seven types of rules describes how the participants are supposed to react to particular types of events, and hence structures the action situation. They are as follows (Crawford and Ostrom 1995; Elinor Ostrom 2010a):

1. *Boundary rules* specify under what conditions a person can occupy a given position, for example who is eligible for various types of positions;
2. *Position rule*s specify the set of positions and how many actors hold each one;

3. *Choice rules* specify the rights and obligations assigned to an actor in each given position and the conditions under which they are allowed to get involved;
4. *Information rules* specify what information must, may, or must not be shared and in what fashion;
5. *Scope rules* restrict actions depending on current observed outcomes, for example "[r]ules that specify that the water stored behind a reservoir may not be released for irrigation if the level falls below the level required for navigation or for generating power" (Elinor Ostrom, Gardner, and Walker 1994, 42).
6. *Aggregation rules* specify the level of consent required to take various collective decisions, e.g. majority or unanimity rules;
7. *Payoff rules* specify how benefits and costs are distributed to actors in various positions.

If you recall, one of the issues raised with respect to Elinor Ostrom's "design principles" was that they might be incomplete. These rules structuring the action situation may give us some hints with respect to what might be missing. They may help us generate more hypotheses about additional "design principles," which may then be empirically evaluated.

In Ostrom's framework, *social reality is the sum of all existing action arenas*. The IAD framework allows us to pack and, when necessary, unpack a tremendous amount of institutional complexity. The complexity results from the fact that the same person may be acting in different action arenas at the same time, that is, have more than just one institutional position, for example, one is both a business owner and the friend of a politician. The IAD framework creates the possibility of building a sufficiently simplified picture for a particular aspect of a matter, while, at the same time, always maintaining the possibility of going into more details. This is possible *because the action arena at one level can be treated as a unit at a higher level.*

For example, we can describe a complex economic system as being made up of a collection of interacting markets. A market can thus be described as an abstract participant (or "sector") in the action arena of the overall economy. Notice, however, that we're not describing a market as an agent with goals and beliefs (i.e., we're not anthropomorphizing it), but as an action arena with internal patterns of interactions and external outcomes. Suppose, however, that we want more details.

Each market itself is also an action arena populated by firms specialized in that market and regulated by various governmental agencies and civil society mechanisms. The participants on a market are thus firms, organizations, and governments. But each of these participants can itself be further described as an action arena made up of other participants such as departments in a corporation or in a governmental agency. Furthermore, these departments (or, in simpler cases, the firms and organizations themselves) are action arenas made of individual firm employees and government bureaucrats. We, thus, see how the language of action arenas allows us to impose structure on a very complex social–institutional reality.

## Evaluation of Outcomes

The purpose of the evaluation is to analyze what happens within an action arena and to compare the result of this analysis with a set of normative goals. Importantly, the evaluation, and subsequent redesign of some of the rules, is not necessarily done by an external agent. In most cases, it is the participants within the action arena who evaluate the outcomes and change the rules. We have seen this in Chapter 3 when we analyzed how people escape the prisoners' dilemma and other "perverse spontaneous orders."

The evaluation is a three-step process:

1. One must first identify the possible and the likely *patterns of interactions* between the actors within their action situation. The likelihood of various courses of action is determined by analyzing the participants' incentive structures—the opportunities they have and the cost of various courses of action. This is analyzed relative to their likely goals.

The patterns of interactions can often be evaluated via algebraic, game theoretical or agent-based modeling approaches (Elinor Ostrom, Gardner, and Walker 1994; Costanza et al. 2000; Elinor Ostrom 2005a; Poteete, Janssen, and Ostrom 2010). However, sometimes the situation can be too complicated for such mathematical approaches, in which case one has to rely on a less rigorous, but not necessarily less reliable, narrative-based analysis of the incentive structure and its consequences (Tarko 2015b).

Underpinning this mode of analysis is the public choice approach focused on the incentives and knowledge of the participants. The public choice analysis, carefully taking into account everyone's incentives and capacity to work toward the stated goal, rather than naively assuming benevolence and overestimating knowledge, explains why the departure from self-governance tends to lead to failure on broader performance criteria. Consider again the case of the irrigation systems, which Elinor Ostrom has studied extensively across the world. She summarized these studies in the following fashion:

> The incentives facing farmers, villagers, and officials are more important in determining long-term performance than is the engineering of the physical systems. When farmers select—and compensate—their own officials to govern and manage an irrigation system that the farmers own and operate, the incentives faced by the officials are closely aligned to the incentives faced by farmers in the system, while the performance of the system is linked to that of the officials. In many centralized, national government systems, no such linkage exists. (Elinor Ostrom, interviewed by Aligica 2003)

She was critical of various outside interventions on the ground that these interventions often do not properly account for the possibly negative changes they spur in the patterns of interactions within the action arena. Or, as V. Ostrom (1980) put it, "human beings are never perfectly obedient automata. Whenever discretion is exercised individuals can be expected to consider their own interests in the actions they take."

2. The second step of the evaluation involves the assessment of the specific aggregate *outcomes*, with regard to the resource/s of interest, that result from the patterns of interaction. Is the resource depleted? It is underutilized? Who uses it and for what purpose? What alternative outcomes are possible, that is, what is the opportunity cost of the prevailing pattern of interactions?

3. Finally, the last step of the evaluation involves a *normative input*. Ideally, this should be the only place where normative matters enter the picture. The normative criteria are used to evaluate the outcomes. Many normative criteria can be considered important, and some tradeoffs between them may be necessary. Resilience is one possible normative criterion. Others can be economic efficiency, fairness, participation rate, etc.

The end result of the evaluation process is the attempted redesign of some of the institutional factors, such that the normative criteria are better satisfied. The main problem of course is that the redesign of the institutional factors is not done by omniscient, impartial, and benevolent agents, but by self-interested actors who try to change the rules and attributes of various institutional positions in the direction that most benefits them, while coping as best as they can with their limited knowledge. Also the redesigning is best understood as being done by (some of) the participants in the action arena, rather than by some outside actor.

## EXAMPLE: SOCIOECOLOGICAL RESILIENCE

To make this framework less abstract, let us consider the example of analyzing the interactions between a community and its natural environment. Costanza, Low, E. Ostrom, and Wilson (2000) pointed out that we need to map out several key elements of this relationship: flows (harvest, pollution, enhancement, nonconsumptive uses), controls (transformations, transactions), and attributes (excludability, observability, knowledge, enforceability, divisibility, sustainability, equity, efficiency). Janssen, Anderies, and E. Ostrom (2004) further developed the framework for analyzing socioecological robustness based on the theoretical insight of the "highly optimized tolerance" (HOT) process discussed in Chapter 4. They then tested this preliminary theoretical framework against additional empirical studies in order to better establish the validity of the HOT perspective. This is the approach of Janssen, Anderies, and E. Ostrom (2007) . Let us now translate all this work into the general IAD language by looking at the details of the *institutional factors* and of the *possible events*. This translation is important because it allows us to fully appreciate the social–institutional aspect of the problem and to see how the relationship to the environment is embedded in society at large.

### Institutional Factors

The first key aspect to clarifying the issue of socioecological robustness within the IAD framework is to determine the relevant institutional factors (Figure 5.5). These lead to a certain conceptualization of the action

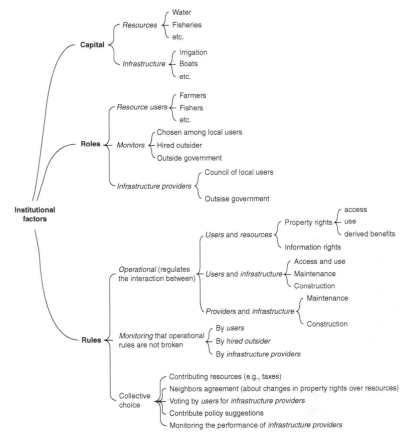

**Figure 5.5. Institutional Factors Relevant for Social–Ecological Resilience. (Adapted from Janssen, Anderies, and E. Ostrom 2004, and Ostrom 2014.)**

arena and thus allow us to gauge the patterns of interactions between the participants and their impact upon the resources. Janssen, Anderies, and Ostrom (2004) consider two types of capital: the physical resource (water, fisheries, etc.) and the infrastructure (irrigation, boats, etc.). There are three institutional roles: resource users (farmers, fishers, etc.), monitors, and public infrastructure providers (council of local users or outside government). There are three types of relevant rules-in-use (also known as "social capital"): operational (regulating the interaction between agents and the resource, and the interaction between agents and the infrastructure), monitoring that the operational rules are not broken, and collective choice rules (establishing the relationship between users and public infrastructure providers).

The operational rules for users with regard to the resource define the users' property rights. The operational rules for either users or providers with regard to the infrastructure may include obligations to contribute to building the infrastructure, and its latter maintenance. The monitoring can be conducted either by users or by the infrastructure providers. Finally, the collective choice rules involve voting for providers, contributing resources (e.g., taxes), offering suggestions for improved policies, and monitoring the performance of the providers. We see the circular aspect of the organization, as opposed to the strictly hierarchical, which is designed to lead to the creation of legitimate rules and to create a vested interest in monitors for doing their job as monitors properly. This reduces the negative public choice effects that follow from having certain people in positions of authority and, thus, potentially, creating the opportunity for abuses and for unfairness.

## The Action Arena

Within the action arena there are a number of possible situations (Figure 5.6). There may be an external ecological disturbance affecting the resource or the infrastructure; external social disturbances affecting either the users or the providers. Internally, there is the users' regular harvesting activity; the providers building and maintaining the infrastructure, perhaps in collaboration with the users; the monitoring of users' harvesting activity; the monitoring of the providers' activity with regard to building and maintaining the infrastructure; and the collective choice process.

In order to analyze the resilience of the system one has to compare the possible external disturbances to the rules that govern the internal activities and asses the weak points of those rules. In other words, one has to see in what ways the internal rules hamper the rapid reaction and/ or adaptation to various possible external disturbances. In order to asses this issue one needs to consider different attributes of these interactions (Costanza et al. 2000, 19–20):

> *Excludability* refers to the capability and cost of keeping some individuals from benefiting from a system.

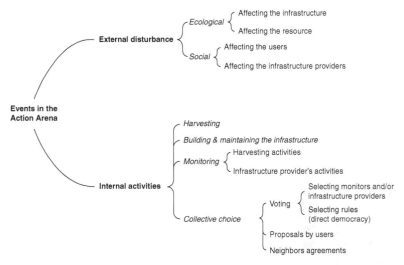

Figure 5.6.   Events in the Action Arena. (Adapted from Janssen, Anderies, and E. Ostrom 2004.)

*Observability* is the capability of detecting and measuring human actions and their consequences on ecosystems and human systems.

*Knowledge* represents the level of understanding of how the system is structured and the relevant values of key variables by those using a particular resource system. . . .

*Enforceability* reflects the feasibility and cost of achieving conformance to rules.

*Divisibility* refers to the separability of a resource into units that can be used by different individuals . . . or the rivalry for the benefits produced.

*Sustainability* . . . reflects the persistence of a stock over time as it is used.

## Patterns of Interactions and the Evaluation of Outcomes

Janssen, Anderies, and Ostrom (2004) identify several kinds of possible problems related to each situation in the action arena. The external disturbances may destroy the resource or the infrastructure. The external social disturbances may lead to conflict, uncertainty, migration, or greatly increased demand. The harvesting activity may be inefficient either due to overharvesting or underharvesting. With regard to the infrastructure, the misallocation of capital may be an issue (either overcapitalization or undercapitalization); the infrastructure may be inefficient, disrupting the spatiotemporal patterns of harvesting and causing unintended consequences; power relations may generate unfair opportunities to use the infrastructure. If users are involved in building and maintaining the infrastructure, free-riding may be a problem. With regard to the issue of monitoring, corruption may be a problem leading to an idiosyncratic enforcement of the operational rules. Finally, with regard to the collective choice process, the participation rate may be low, accurate information may be lacking, agenda setting may distort the process, and rent-seeking may lead to unfair advantages.

The point of the evaluation is that, depending on the negative outcomes, the participants can cooperate to change the rules described above. Moreover, as discussed in Chapter 4, resilience depends on the capacity to alter the rules in response to changes in the environmental conditions. In other words, it depends on the capacity to adapt to changing circumstances. This brings us back to Hamilton's question from *Federalist 1* about "whether societies of men are really capable or not of establishing good government from reflection and choice, or whether they are forever destined to depend for their political constitutions on accident and force."

## INSTITUTIONAL EVOLUTION AND PUBLIC ENTREPRENEURSHIP

Elinor Ostrom (2014) adopts an evolutionary approach to institutions, but at the same time departs in a very significant fashion from other, more well-known approaches to cultural evolution (Boyd and Richerson 1988; Dennett 1995, pt. 3; Sperber 1996; Richerson and Boyd 2006). Following Hayek (1989), she is weary of what people imagine they can design, but, unlike the authors just mentioned, she does not adopt the radical stance of assuming that rules and norms vary *at random*. This is the main critique that Hayek's own account of institutional evolution has received (Buchanan 1977).

When creating a cultural evolutionary model one must specify three things: (1) what varies, (2) what is the mechanism that generates the variation, and (3) what are the selection criteria that preserve some variations and discard others. We have already briefly discussed the evaluation of outcomes, which corresponds to the selection mechanism in the evolutionary process. Let us look at the other two.

## Rules as the Basic Unit of Institutional Evolution

With regard to the first point—what varies?—E. Ostrom makes an analogy between biological evolution and institutional evolution, pointing out that rules and norms are the equivalent of genes, while the resulting society with its incentives structures is the equivalent of the phenotype (Elinor Ostrom 2014):

> Self-organizing resource governance systems have two structures that are somewhat parallel in their function to the concepts of a genotype and a phenotype in biological systems. The genotypic structure characterizes the set of instructions encoded in DNA to produce an organism with a particular phenotypic structure. Phenotypic structures characterize an *expressed organism*—how bones, organs, and muscles develop, relate, and function in an organism in a particular environment.
>
> A rule configuration is parallel in function to a genotype. It is a set of instructions of how to produce the expressed situation or the structure of relationships among individuals that is also affected by the biophysical world and the kind of community or culture in which an action situation is located. The components of an action situation (or a game) characterize an *expressed situation* [corresponding to the phenotype]—how the number of participants, the information available, and their opportunities and costs create incentives, and how incentives lead to types of outcomes in a particular environment.

This is an important point because it frames the issue of cultural evolution as a competition between different systems of rules and norms, rather than a competition between people themselves (subjected to those rules and norms). Rules and norms are often described as tools used by communities to achieve various goals. But, in the cultural evolution perspective, communities are not necessarily seen as being in conflict with one another over access to various scarce resources, and the rules and norms are not merely weapons in such conflicts. While *some* norms and rules might have such utility, most of them do not. Thus, systems of rules and norms are in competition with one another even in the absence of any conflict between the communities that have the norms and rules. Thus, the competition between systems of rules and norms is more general than the competition between persons (legal persons and physical persons) or communities.

## Public Entrepreneurship

With regard to point 2—what drives the variation?—E. Ostrom points out that the variation of rules and norms is often the result of rational design, rather than mere randomness, and that there often are metarules (such as constitutions) about how the rules are to be changed:

> Some changes in rules—such as those resulting from memory loss—may resemble blind variation. Instead of relying entirely on blind variation, however, human agents frequently try to use reason and persuasion in their efforts to devise better rules (for themselves and their supporters or for a broader community). The process of choice, however, always involves experimentation. Self-organized resource governance systems use many types of decision rules to make collective choices ranging from deferring to the judgment of one person or elders, to using majority voting, to relying on unanimity. (Elinor Ostrom 2014)

The main effect of such departures from mere randomness is that the speed of development can be much faster and societies can, to some extent, overcome path dependencies. While evolution by blind variation and natural selection only tinkers with existing designs, rational variation can involve radical redesigns.

> Participants adapt the rules, norms, and strategies of their parents and elders as well as those who are viewed as highly successful in a particular culture. They learn from neighboring systems that work better than theirs and try to discern which rules are helping their neighbors to do better. Human agents try to use reason and persuasion in their efforts to devise better rules, but the process of choice from the vast array of rules they might use always involves experimentation. (Elinor Ostrom 2005a, 244)

It is for this reason that the Bloomington School departs in a significant way from other public choice approaches by giving a far greater emphasis on the role of ideas. Vincent Ostrom (1993) referred to this as the issue of "epistemic choice," meaning that our theories of collective action are incomplete if we only look at incentive problems. We also need to understand how ideas take over a society, sometimes generating radical institutional changes (Tarko 2015c).

The alternative to changing institutions by "accident or force" is to understand such changes as driven by a certain type of entrepreneurship, but in the public sphere rather than in the private (Elinor Ostrom 1965, 2005b; Oakerson and Parks 1988). This idea has received quite a lot of attention more recently both on theoretical grounds (Boettke and Coyne 2009a, 2009b; Leeson and Boettke 2009), and as an empirical tool for understanding the differences in recovery rates of different communities from Hurricane Katrina (Chamlee-Wright and Storr 2009, 2010a, 2010b; Grube and Storr 2013; N. M. Storr, Chamlee-Wright, and Storr 2015).

This literature makes two important points. On one hand, especially in the context of polycentricity, we can see public entrepreneurship as a complement to Tiebout competition (Oakerson and Parks 1988). In the original model of interjurisdictional competition, Tiebout had made the simplifying assumption of perfect competition. This is obviously far from realistic, and once Tiebout and Vincent Ostrom got together working on the Lakewood Project (see Chapter 1), one of their main concerns was to develop an oligopolistic model of interjurisdictional competition. Ronald Oakerson's and Roger Parks' (1988) article on public entrepreneurship in the metropolitan areas can be seen as the culmination of this approach. They noted that not only are jurisdictions not perfectly competitive (due to the existence of often prohibitive exit costs), but also the officials, who might be out of office after a few years, lack the incentives for long-term planning. This makes the market-like constraints upon the local public administrations, due to the possibility of citizens (and firms) leaving, quite weak—certainly much weaker than the constraints faced by firms on regular markets due to the possibility of customers switching to other firms.

This leads us back to the emphasis on coproduction and civil society pressures upon the public administration, what Hirschman (1970) has called "voice." In other words, public entrepreneurship works better when citizens play a part in the co-production of rule changes (Aligica and Tarko 2013). Otherwise, the imperfections of Tiebout competition will lead officials to be relatively unresponsive to citizens' needs.

The recent literature on the Katrina recovery brings further empirical evidence in favor of the same idea. What the teams coordinated by Emily Chamlee-Wright and Virgil Storr have discovered was that civil society "social entrepreneurs" played a vital part in the recovery process. They note that recovery after a massive hurricane has the incentive structure of a tragedy of the commons (see chapter 3): People were willing to return and rebuild only if others did the same. The problem is that everyone had the incentive to wait until the others had returned, and no one had the incentive to return first. What they discovered was that the escape from this dilemma was possible thanks to community coordinators, such as priests who kept track of the members of the community, contacted them trying to persuade them to return, and who were able to assure the members of the community that many others will return as well.

This highlights the other important point of this literature on public entrepreneurship: the task of such entrepreneurs is usually to provide some focal points for coordination. As Vincent Ostrom put it:

> Organizations are instruments or tools that enable human beings to engage in forms of joint [institutional] artisanship.... This implies some basic calculations made by artisans in creating artifacts must be jointly made by a number of individuals where division of labor in the joint effort may imply that no two persons jointly involved make precisely the same calculations. *Underlying the joint endeavor is the need for a shared understanding of the joint task that enables human beings to coordinate their actions with one another.* Yet, each is an artisan accountable to his own sense of artisanship as he functions in the joint endeavor. (V. Ostrom 1980, emphasis added)

These public entrepreneurs help create what Vincent Ostrom (1997) has called "shared communities of understanding." By creating focal points for coordination, they diminish the heterogeneity of *both* preferences and beliefs: "social change involves both an act of creation and one of convergence ... not just creating a new focal point but also developing common knowledge to make it focal on a larger scale" (Boettke and Coyne 2009a). At least to some extent, individual preferences are endogenously created by such social processes, which, in turn, can lead to significant political consequences. As Elinor Ostrom has noted,

> In complex situations involving unstructured problems, assuming complete preference functions of any shape is not meaningful. The most one

can say is that the individuals in such situations are engaged in a trial-and-error effort to learn more about the results of their actions so that they can evaluate the benefits and costs more effectively over time. (Elinor Ostrom 1990, 38)

Following this line of thought, theories of public entrepreneurship try to explain how the public agenda gets created as a prerequisite for then trying to solve the problems. The presence of such entrepreneurs makes social coordination easier than one might believe just from a fixed preferences account, because of the possibility of convergence upon a set of common values. Furthermore, ideas come to serve as focal points, and ideas guide actions, including attempts at changing the institutional framework, and influence the way in which people interpret their private interests (López & Leighton 2012; Storr 2015; Tarko 2015c).

This being said, as Boettke and Coyne (2009a) note, we should not forget the public choice skepticism toward assuming too much benevolence. One can provide an entrepreneurial theory of social change by mapping the *personal* benefits that these public entrepreneurs can get as a result of becoming focal points and facilitating the emergence of a certain uniformity of values and beliefs. The social entrepreneurs who create successful focal points "gain a 'profit' via increased reputation capital," while "those that fail to meet consumer needs incur a 'loss' via decreased reputation capital" (Boettke and Coyne 2009a).

A relatively less-studied area is under what conditions the social entrepreneurs may make things worse rather than better. Different individuals speculating the possibility of creating different focal points for coordination can lead to the emergence of new important institutional roles. Because all rules need enforcement, the creation of all institutional arrangements involves "Faustian bargains where instruments of evil are used to do good. Those who have legitimate access to use such instruments of evil have unique opportunities to exploit others and dominate the allocation of values in a society" (V. Ostrom 1980). Institutional roles are created because they enable societies to do a lot more things, but then regulations are often needed to curtail the abuses of power made possible by the very creation of institutional roles.

## Coproduction

The above discussion highlights the interplay between the public entrepreneurs and the citizens. To make this relationship more precise, the

Bloomington School developed the concept of coproduction (Parks et al. 1981; Percy 1984; Elinor Ostrom 1996; Aligica and Tarko 2013). This concept is an important theoretical extension of standard economic theory. What became obvious in all these CPR studies was that *the consumer was often part of the production process*—which meant that the standard economic separation between the producer who sells a product and the consumer who buys it was not tenable.

Once one understands this idea of a "consumer producer" (i.e., a consumer actively implicated in the production process, but who, nonetheless, pays something to the "regular producer," with whom s/he cooperates, for the product), one starts to see it everywhere: A video game doesn't entertain without being played; a concert is not a success if the public is completely passive; a professor cannot teach an unwilling or completely apathetic student; a doctor often needs the patient's inputs in the process of diagnosis; the police cannot catch criminals if citizens are unwilling to provide them with any clues; fire protection services depend on the citizens' efforts to prevent fires; the justice system cannot function if no one is willing to be a witness, etc.

Elinor Ostrom and her collaborators first became aware of the importance of coproduction in their police studies. They have noticed that "[l]ocking doors, avoiding certain areas and activities, respecting others' property, treating neighbors with dignity and respect, and a willingness to work with the police in reporting and identifying wrong-doers in the community all impact the measured effectiveness of police outputs on public safety" (Boettke, Palagashvili, and Lemke 2013). Trying to understand the ways in which "producers and consumers of the public good must work in tandem in order to generate the desired outcome" (Boettke, Palagashvili, and Lemke 2013) they noticed that they were moving beyond the standard consumer theory framework. As a result, they created a similar, but different, basic mathematical model of coproduction (Parks et al. 1981).

From this model it follows that, when the regular producer and the consumer producer are interdependent, as in the cases mentioned above, a trade-off emerges between the efforts of the regular producer and of the consumer producer (Figure 5.7). The resulting outcome, how much is produced and what is the relative involvement of the two parts, depends on the relative costs encountered by them: the production costs (wages, etc.) paid by the regular producer versus the opportunity

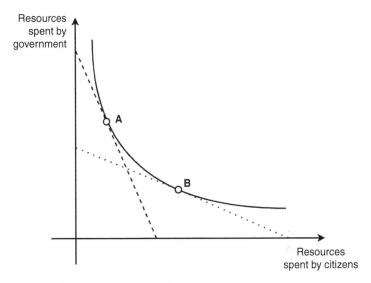

**Figure 5.7.   The Coproduction of a Public Service.**

cost of the consumer to get involved in the production process (what alternative benefits s/he could have by spending his or her time differently). In Figure 5.7, the solid line describes the production function for a given public service. This production function has two inputs: the resources spent by the government and the resources contributed by the citizens. Two different cases, with different coproduction equilibria are illustrated. The dashed line reflects a situation in which the opportunity costs of citizens' participation are relatively high. As a result, citizens are relatively little involved. By contrast, the dotted line describes a situation in which the opportunity costs of citizens' participation are relatively low. These opportunity costs may be not just due to income, but also due to different preferences. Somewhat unintuitively, they have found that

citizens do not share similar preferences for ... urban goods and services. The preferences of citizens living in relatively poorer neighborhoods differ substantially from those living in wealthier neighborhoods. In regard to recreational services, for example, residents living in neighborhoods where private living space is crowded have strong preferences for the use of public spaces—urban streets as well as parks—to be used as safe gathering places and for sports. Citizens living in wealthier neighborhoods, on the other hand, have a strong preference for quiet public spaces; they use private space for recreation. (Elinor Ostrom 2000)

As Aligica and Boettke (2009, 33) note, "[t]he role of co-production came in many respects as a revelation," as it became obvious that the analysis of many public services was deficient because it ignored this issue. "[O]nce it was clearly defined, co-production problems could be identified in many sub-domains of the service industries in both private and public sectors. ... It was the standard assumption of the separation of production from consumption that blinded everybody from identifying the source of what was called the 'service paradox.'"

The "service paradox" consists in a situation in which "[t]he better services are, as defined by professional criteria, the less satisfied the citizens are with those services" (V. Ostrom and Ostrom 1977). This paradox emerges when the evaluation of the production process focuses solely on the part provided by the regular producer, ignoring the part played by the consumer producer. Consequently, in such cases, the coproduction trade-off is drifting away from its optimum and the interaction between the two parts is becoming more and more defective despite the genuine efforts to improve the service. To give a simple example, education may turn to the worse despite genuine improvements of textbooks and of classrooms materials, if the student motivation aspects of the education process are not properly addressed. Similarly, if we see democracy as the coproduction of rules (Aligica and Tarko 2013), the performance of the public sector can suffer as we move toward a greater focus on "expert"-driven reforms and leaving less and less room for regular citizens' inputs.

One of the possible problems in systems depending on coproduction is that the public sector may free-ride to some extent on the citizens' involvement or, conversely, the citizens may shirk their civic duties by overly relying on the government to do most of the work. This is similar to a team-production problem within firms and organization, where workers may shirk and free-ride on other workers' efforts, but with an importance difference: While in the case of team production, the good is produced for outsider consumers, in the case of coproduction, citizens actually have a vested interest in the good being produced because they themselves are the consumers. Aligica and Tarko (2013) note that the conceptual confusion between team production and coproduction leads to significant errors because the solution to team-production problems within firms is to have a hierarchical organization with higher level managers monitoring the workers (Alchian and Demsetz 1972). By contrast, hierarchical attempts to solve coproduction free-riding problems are bound to make matters worse because the higher level monitors do not have a similar vested interest in the production of the good as citizens do. Consequently, the solution to coproduction problems needs to be self-governance and building trust between the community and the officials (Aligica and Tarko 2013). Thus, confusing coproduction problems with team-production problems leads us to attempt a wrong-headed solution leading to overcentralization and greater disconnect between citizens and government. To reiterate Elinor Ostrom's warning,

> officials and policy analysts who presume that they have the right design can be dangerous. They are likely to assume that citizens are short-sighted and motivated only by extrinsic benefits and costs. Somehow, the officials and policy analysts assume that they have different motivations and can find optimal policy because they are not directly involved in the problem .... They are indeed isolated from the problems. This leaves them with little capability to adapt and learn in light of information about outcomes resulting from their policies. All too often, these "optimal" policies have Leviathan-like characteristics to them. (Elinor Ostrom 2005a, 256)

## BUILDING A SCIENCE OF ASSOCIATION

The bottom line of this whole approach is that if we are to understand how societies can establish good rules by reflection and choice, rather than by accident and force, we need to better understand how public entrepreneurship operates. In order to understand how such entrepreneurship operates, we need to bear in mind the distinction between organizations (which can be reasonably described as pursuing specific "missions" and having "beliefs" about what means best serve their ends), and more complex institutional arrangements which cannot be anthropomorphized.

The Ostroms have long claimed that states, governments, societies, and markets are *not* organizations (in Douglass North's sense) and we talk about them as if they are at our peril. How should we think about such complex institutions? The Bloomington School developed the IAD framework precisely for this purpose. Describing complex institutions as collections of action arenas, which generate observable outcomes as a result of their internal patterns of interactions, can help us overcome the temptation to apply the intentional stance to everything. Thinking in terms of simplified action arenas, which focus our attention of smaller groups of people dealing with specific problems, can also help us simplify an otherwise bewildering situation. Practitioners have, indeed, found this framework very useful precisely for this reason, in particular for the task of understanding the interactions between communities and their natural environment.

But, on a broader note, the Ostroms also believed that using such a nonanthropomorphic framework may help citizens better understand their world and be more effective in changing it. In other words, it may help further develop the Tocquevillian art and science of association (Boettke, Lemke, and Palagashvili 2014).

Robert Bish (2014) noted that the Ostroms' project tried to respond to two forms of pessimism, one from Max Weber about the inevitability of hierarchical bureaucratic organizations, and one from Alexis de Tocqueville about the collapse of democracies due to the gradual loss of civic virtues. On the first one,

> Weber observed that in operation, a bureaucracy becomes rigid, mechanical, and unable to adapt to changing conditions. It is not an ideal way to organize government. In contrast, his model of democratic administration is more responsive to citizens and more adaptable. However, in spite of the desirable characteristics of democratic administration, Weber believed it was not feasible on a large scale, but rather had to be limited to smaller governments. He was pessimistic about large-scale bureaucracies, but did not believe there was an alternative. Weber did not seem to have contemplated Vincent's polycentricity, or federalism, as the way to govern a large society. (Bish 2014)

The whole point of the research on polycentricity was, indeed, to show, first, that, empirically speaking, large-scale governments *are not in fact* hierarchical, but polycentric, and, second, that, from a normative point of view, we *should not* try to turn them into hierarchical organizations. We can say that, although this point is still not widely understood, they did nonetheless successfully counter Weber's pessimism. The bureaucratic administration is not an inevitability, but a *choice* made due to a misunderstanding of the nature of complex institutions. Which brings us to the second issue:

Tocqueville did not believe citizens understand how democratic administration and multicentered systems work; hence, citizens seek solutions to problems with a single-sovereign bureaucratic approach. Tocqueville believed that the faith in single-sovereign solutions would eventually suffocate the energy of citizens and destroy democratic administration. (Bish 2014)

The Ostroms indeed took this possibility very seriously (V. Ostrom 1997; Vincent and Elinor Ostrom, interviewed by Aligica 2003). Bish recalls that

Vincent was concerned with what he perceived to be a decline in public participation in civic life, something that went beyond simply participation in governance, and the increasing nationalization of activities that had formerly been left to civic associations or state and local government where citizen participation was much more likely. (Bish 2014)

Their attempt to counteract this tendency ranged from their police and water management studies in the United States and to the management of CPRs across the world. The creation of the IAD framework, while serving direct practical uses, is also an attempt to build a conceptual alternative to the "single-sovereign" understanding of all problems. The study of CPRs was part of this broader concern with Tocquevillian self-governance: "My hope is…that the examination and analysis of CPRs in the field, in the experimental laboratory, and in theory, contribute to the development of an empirically valid theory of self-organization and self-governance" (Elinor Ostrom, interviewed by Aligica 2003). As Robert Bish (2014) rightly notes,

[t]he most important scholar in the development of a science of association to counter the single-sovereign model had been Elinor Ostrom. Elinor led empirical work worldwide, beginning with her dissertation, studies of citizen perceptions of their local services, and the largest-scale study of a public service industry, policing, that has been done in the United States. After that, most of her work was on natural resources and commons problems.

As the Bloomington School continues after Elinor and Vincent Ostrom's departure, the major challenge still continues:

A Tocquevillian science of association—a body of knowledge that helps us to understand the nature of social order, and the forms of social interaction that lead to mutual advantage—is the foundation for choosing among the institutional alternatives open to us. Now, it remains to be determined whether human beings can actually use such methods of discussion, reflection, and choice to fashion the future course of human civilization. (Vincent Ostrom, interviewed by Aligica 2003)

# Conclusion

## *Elinor Ostrom as a Role Model for Social Scientists*

Lin Ostrom stands as an exemplar of the "scholar entrepreneur." Throughout her career, Lin has been pathbreaking in her willingness to embrace academic advances across disciplines and methodologies. She has authored or coauthored hundreds of scientific papers that incorporate cutting-edge methods across all of the social sciences, as well as the natural sciences (Poteete, Janssen, and Ostrom 2010). In addition to her early focus on police institutions and field studies, her work with collaborators includes some of the earliest analyses of CPR issues in game theory and experimental methods, as well as more recent use of agent-based modeling techniques and geographic information systems. She adeptly uses all of these diverse tools and approaches to explore one central theme: how individuals, groups, and communities have used their capacity for self-governance to craft institutional arrangements that enable them to effectively cope with perverse economic and social incentives that threaten to undermine their ability to survive. (McGinnis and Walker 2010)

Elinor Ostrom's success, both as an individual scientist and as an organizer of a major research center, has grown out of particularly tolerant attitude toward methodology. She pragmatically embraced multiple methods of doing research, going from game theory modeling all the way to narrative case studies. She was never shy about the fact that her methodology ran against the pure strictures of "positivism." From an important article in the early 1980s called "Beyond positivism" to one of her last coauthored books, *Working Together*, she emphasized the role of theory in providing suggestions about empirical research (as was

*Photo 7. Elinor and Vincent Ostrom, Manitoulin Island, 1968 (Elinor Ostrom Collection, The Lilly Library)*

the case with her empirical police studies being provoked by Vincent Ostrom's theoretical arguments) and the value of multiple methods (as was the case with her work on the commons which relied on everything from case studies to game theory).

One way of thinking about methodology is to note that "models serve as 'substitute systems' of the target systems they represent" and that "systems in the real world are characteristically all too complex to be tractable targets for direct examination, therefore they are represented by much simpler model systems" (Mäki 2005). Consequently, different types of models will abstract from reality in different ways, and each approach will have certain strengths and weaknesses. When dealing with complex problems, one is bound to need a diversity of methods, and "[i]t is important for social scientists to recognize that all methods generate results that contain some level of uncertainty" (Poteete, Janssen, and Ostrom 2010, 4). Rather than deciding which method is "the best" and reject all others in its favor, we are better off considering the comparative advantages of a variety of methods, and adopt what Oliver Williamson (2009), Elinor's Nobel corecipient has called a "pragmatic methodology," which tries to "keep it simple; get it right; make it plausible":

> Keeping it simple is accomplished by stripping away inessentials, thereby to focus on first order effects—the main case, as it were—after which qualifications, refinements and extensions can be introduced. Getting it right entails working out the logic. And making it plausible means to preserve contact with the phenomena and eschew fanciful constructions.

All too often, social scientists overly constrain themselves to one single method and, hence, miss out on possible discoveries. When we take the "community" part of the scientific community seriously, we are led to wonder how Elinor Ostrom's design principles apply to it as well. Her warning against "blueprint thinking" thus finds a not-too-subtle echo in her methodological pragmatism. In particular, the focus on econometric analysis as the sole approach to empirical analysis is questionable (Labrousse 2016). When setting up such an analysis, we need to bear in mind that "additional variables consume degrees of freedom in a context of limited data availability," that "[t]he assumption that observations are independent ... is called into question by globalization, diffusion effects, and actor-centered theories that emphasize strategic interactions," and that it is often the case that "interaction effects, dummy variables, hierarchical models, and other similar statistical fixes do not accurately reflect the relationships posited in the underlying theories" (Poteete, Janssen, and Ostrom 2010, 13).

Echoing Hayek's (1989) Nobel address about the economists' "pretense of knowledge," Elinor Ostrom summarized the challenges created by the study of complex social systems in the following way:

> It is now obvious that the search for rules that will improve institutions and government is not as straightforward as many scholars—some of them not at all utopian and naïve—were once inclined to believe.... Because multiple rules affect each of the many components of a particular setting, conducting ... a complete analysis would involve more time and resources than many policy analysts have assumed in the past.

Instead of assuming that designing effective governance systems is a relatively simple analytical task that can be undertaken by a team of objective analysts sitting in the national capital, or at an international headquarters, it is important that we understand policy design to require experimentation with combinations of large numbers of component parts (Elinor Ostrom, interviewed by Aligica 2003).

And looking back to her research agenda, analyzing local public economies and analyzing common-pool resources, she drew the following conclusions (Elinor Ostrom 2000):

> From my participation in these two extended research programs, I have learned to be skeptical whenever I hear the phrase "it is self-evident" that some empirical regularity occurs in a sociopolitical setting. ~~Patterns of relationships among individuals and groups tend to be relatively complex and rarely lend themselves to simple explanations~~. Reforms based on overly simplified views of the world have led to counterintuitive and counterintentional results in both urban and CPR environments.

Further, I have gained an ever greater respect for polycentric systems and the direct involvement of citizens in governance. While all institutions are subject to takeover by opportunistic individuals and to the potential for perverse dynamics, a political system that has multiple centers of power at differing scales provides more opportunity for citizens and their officials to innovate and to intervene so as to correct maldistributions of authority and outcomes. Thus, ~~polycentric systems are more likely than monocentric systems to provide incentives leading to self-organized, self-corrective institutional change~~. Trying to understand how complex multicentered, multilevel political systems operate is difficult. Thus, theoretically driven empirical research is an essential element of improving the operation of a democratic system. Empirically supported theories are important tools for the effective conduct of policy analysis and the successful reform of political systems.

# References

Adger, W. Neil. 2006. "Vulnerability." *Global Environmental Change* 16(3): 268–81.

Alchian, Armen A., and Harold Demsetz. 1972. "Production, Information Costs, and Economic Organization." *American Economic Review* 62(5): 777–95.

———. 1973. "The Property Right Paradigm." *Journal of Economic History* 33(1): 16–27.

Aligica, Paul Dragos. 2003. *Rethinking Institutional Analysis: Interviews with Vincent and Elinor Ostrom with Introductions by Vernon Smith and Gordon Tullock*. Mercatus Center. Whasington, DC.

———. 2013. *Institutional Diversity and Political Economy: The Ostroms and Beyond*. Oxford and New York: Oxford University Press.

Aligica, Paul Dragos, and Peter J. Boettke. 2009. *Challenging Institutional Analysis and Development: The Bloomington School*. London and New York: Routledge.

Aligica, Paul Dragos, and Vlad Tarko. 2012. "Polycentricity: From Polanyi to Ostrom, and Beyond." *Governance* 25(2): 237–62.

———. 2013. "Co-Production, Polycentricity, and Value Heterogeneity: The Ostroms' Public Choice Institutionalism Revisited." *American Political Science Review* 107(4): 726–41.

———. 2014a. *Capitalist Alternatives: Models, Taxonomies, Scenarios*. London and New York: Routledge.

———. 2014b. "Crony Capitalism: Rent Seeking, Institutions and Ideology." *Kyklos* 67(2): 156–76.

———. 2014c. "Institutional Resilience and Economic Systems: Lessons from Elinor Ostrom's Work." *Comparative Economic Studies* 56(1): 52–76.

Anderies, John M., and Marco A. Janssen. 2013. "Robustness of Social–Ecological Systems: Implications for Public Policy." *Policy Studies Journal* 41(3): 513–36.

Anderson, William, and Edward W. Weidner. 1950. *American City Government.* New York: Henry Holt & Co.

Aumann, Robert J. 1987. "Correlated Equilibrium as an Expression of Bayesian Rationality." *Econometrica* 55(1): 1–18.

Axelrod, Robert. 1984. *Evolution of Cooperation.* New York: Basic Books.

———. 1997. *The Complexity of Cooperation: Agent-Based Models of Competition and Collaboration.* Princeton, NJ: Princeton University Press.

Bastiat, Frédéric. 1845. *Economic Sophisms.* Irvington-on-Hudson, NY: The Foundation for Economic Education, 1996. Library of Economics and Liberty. http://www.econlib.org/library/Bastiat/basSoph.html.

Baumol, William J. 1996. "Entrepreneurship: Productive, Unproductive, and Destructive." *Journal of Business Venturing* 11(1): 3–22.

Beito, David T. 2000. *From Mutual Aid to the Welfare State: Fraternal Societies and Social Services, 1890–1967.* Chapel Hill: University of North Carolina Press.

Bish, Robert L. 1971. *The Public Economy of the Metropolitan Areas.* Wisbech, United Kingdom: Markham.

———. 1999. "Federalis Theory and Polycentricity: Learning from Local Governments." In *Limiting Leviathan,* ed. Donald P. Racheter and Richard E. Wagner. Cheltenham, UK, and Northampton, MA: Edward Elgar.

———. 2014. "Vincent Ostrom's Contributions to Political Economy." *Publius: Journal of Federalism* 44(2): 227–48.

Bish, Robert L., and Robert J. Kirk. 1974. *Economic Principles and Urban Problems.* Upper Saddle River, NJ: Prentice-Hall.

Bish, Robert L., and Vincent Ostrom. 1973. *Understanding Urban Government: Metropolitan Reform Reconsidered.* American Enterprise Institute for Public Policy Research. Whasington, DC.

Blomquist, William, Edella Schlager, and Tanya Heikkila. 2004. *Common Waters, Diverging Streams: Linking Institutions and Water Management in Arizona, California, and Colorado.* Washington, DC: Routledge.

Bó, Ernesto Dal. 2006. "Regulatory Capture: A Review." *Oxford Review of Economic Policy* 22(2): 203–25.

Boettke, Peter J. 1996. "Why Culture Matters: Economics, Politics, and the Imprint of History." In *Calculation and Coordination.* London and New York: Routledge, 2001, 248–65.

Boettke, Peter J., and Rosolino A. Candela. 2015. "Rivalry, Polycentricism, and Institutional Evolution". *Advances in Austrian Economics*, 19: 1-19.

Boettke, Peter J., and Christopher J. Coyne. 2009a. "An Entrepreneurial Theory of Social and Cultural Change." In *Markets and Civil Society: The European Experience in Comparative Perspective*, ed. Víctor Pérez Díaz. New York: Berghahn Books, 77–103.

———. 2009b. "Context Matters: Institutions and Entrepreneurship." *Foundations and Trends in Entrepreneurship* 5(3): 135–209.

Boettke, Peter J., Christopher J. Coyne, and Peter T. Leeson. 2008. "Institutional Stickiness and the New Development Economics." *American Journal of Economics and Sociology* 67(2): 331–58.

Boettke, Peter J., Jayme S. Lemke, and Liya Palagashvili. 2012. *The Relevance of the Municipality Debate for the Solution of Collective Action Problems*. Arlington, VA: Mercatus Center. GMU Working Paper in Economics No. 12-58. http://papers.ssrn.com/abstract=2175628 (May 13, 2016).

———. 2014. "Polycentricity, Self-Governance, and the Art & Science of Association." *Review of Austrian Economics* 28(3): 311–35.

Boettke, Peter J., Jayme S. Lemke, and Liya Palagashvili. 2016. "Re-Evaluating Community Policing in a Polycentric System." Journal of Institutional Economics 12(2): 305–25.

Boettke, Peter J., Liya Palagashvili, and Jayme Lemke. 2013. "Riding in Cars with Boys: Elinor Ostrom's Adventures with the Police." *Journal of Institutional Economics* 9(4): 407–25.

Boyd, Robert, and Peter J. Richerson. 1988. *Culture and the Evolutionary Process*, 0002 edn. Chicago, IL: University of Chicago Press.

Brentwood, Mary, and Stephen F. Robar, eds. 2004. *Managing Common Pool Groundwater Resources: An International Perspective*. Westport, CT: Greenwood.

Bruns, Bryan Randolph. 2012. "Escaping Prisoner's Dilemmas: From Discord to Harmony in the Landscape of 2 × 2 Games." Working Paper. http://arxiv.org/abs/1206.1880 (May 11, 2016).

———. 2015. "Names for Games: Locating 2 × 2 Games." *Games* 6(4): 495–520.

Buchanan, James M. 1954. "Individual Choice in Voting and the Market." *Journal of Political Economy* 62(4): 334–43.

———. 1965. "An Economic Theory of Clubs." *Economica* 32(125): 1–14.

———. 1968. *The Demand and Supply of Public Goods*. Collected Works of James M. Buchanan, 1999. Indianapolis, IN: Liberty Fund.

———. 1975. "The Samaritan's Dilemma." In *Altruism, Morality and Economic Theory*, ed. Edmund S. Phelps. New York: Russell Sage Foundation, 71–86.

———. 1977. "Law and the Invisible Hand." In *Moral Science and Moral Order*, Indianapolis, IN: Liberty Fund, 2001, 96–109.

———. 1979. *What Should Economists Do?* Indianapolis, IN: Liberty Fund.

———. 1987. "Justification of the Compound Republic: The Calculus in Retrospect." *Cato Journal* 7(2): 305–12.

Buchanan, James M., and Gordon Tullock. 1962. *The Calculus of Consent.* Collected Works of James M. Buchanan, 1999. Indianapolis, IN: Liberty Fund.

Buchanan, James M., Gordon Tullock, and Robert Tollison, eds. 1980. *Toward a Theory of the Rent-Seeking Society.* College Station, TX: Texas A&M University Press.

Buchanan, James M., and Richard E. Wagner. 1977. *Democracy in Deficit.* Collected Works of James M. Buchanan, 2000. Indianapolis, IN: Liberty Fund.

Buck, Susan J. 1998. *The Global Commons: An Introduction,* 2nd edn. Washington, DC: Island Press.

Caplan, Bryan. 2008. *The Myth of the Rational Voter: Why Democracies Choose Bad Policies.* Princeton, NJ, and Woodstock, UK: Princeton University Press.

Carlson, J. M., and John Doyle. 1999. "Highly Optimized Tolerance: A Mechanism for Power Laws in Designed Systems." *Physical Review E* 60(2): 1412–27.

———. 2000. "Highly Optimized Tolerance: Robustness and Design in Complex Systems." *Physical Review Letters* 84(11): 2529–32.

———. 2002. "Complexity and Robustness." *Proceedings of the National Academy of Sciences* 99(suppl 1): 2538–45.

Carnap, Rudolf. 1950. "Empiricism, Semantics, and Ontology." *Revue Internationale de Philosophie* 4(11): 20–40.

CfSR. 2016. "Cost to Consumers." *Coalition for Sugar Reform.* http://sugarreform.org/why-reform/costs-of-the-sugar-program/cost-to-consumers/ (March 18, 2016).

Chamlee-Wright, Emily. 2013. *The Cultural and Political Economy of Recovery: Social Learning in a Post-Disaster Environment.* London and New York: Routledge.

Chamlee-Wright, Emily, and Virgil Henry Storr. 2009. " 'There's No Place Like New Orleans': Sense of Place and Community Recovery in the Ninth Ward after Hurricane Katrina." *Journal of Urban Affairs* 31(5): 615–34.

———, eds. 2010a. *The Political Economy of Hurricane Katrina and Community Rebound.* Cheltenham, UK: Edward Elgar.

———. 2010b. "The Role of Social Entrepreneurship in Post-Katrina Community Recovery." *International Journal of Innovation and Regional Development* 2(1): 149–64.

Coase, Ronald H. 1937. "The Nature of the Firm." *Economica* 4(16): 386–405.

———. 1960. "The Problem of Social Cost." *Journal of Law and Economics* 3: 1–44.

Cole, Daniel H. 2015. "Advantages of a Polycentric Approach to Climate Change Policy." *Nature Climate Change* 5(2): 114–18.

Cole, Daniel H., and Michael D. McGinnis. 2014. *Elinor Ostrom and the Bloomington School of Political Economy, Vol. 1: Polycentricity in Public Administration and Political Science*. Lanham, MD: Lexington Books.

Costanza, Robert, Bobbi Low, Elinor Ostrom, and James Wilson, eds. 2000. *Institutions, Ecosystems, and Sustainability*, 1st edn. Boca Raton: CRC Press.

Cowen, Tyler, ed. 1992. *Public Goods and Market Failures: A Critical Examinations*. New Brunswick, NJ: Transaction.

Cox, Michael E. 2014. "Understanding Large Social–Ecological Systems: Introducing the SESMAD Project." *International Journal of the Commons* 8(2): 265–76.

Cox, Michael E., Gwen Arnold, and Sergio Villamayor Tomás. 2010. "A Review of Design Principles for Community-Based Natural Resource Management." *Ecology and Society* 15(4): 38.

Coyne, Christopher J. 2008. *After War: The Political Economy of Exporting Democracy*. Stanford, CA: Stanford University Press.

———. 2013. *Doing Bad by Doing Good: Why Humanitarian Action Fails*. Stanford, CA: Stanford University Press.

Coyne, Christopher J., and Abigail R. Hall-Blanco. 2016. "Foreign Intervention, Police Militarization, and the Impact on Minority Groups." *Peace Review* (forthcoming). http://papers.ssrn.com/abstract=2729295 (February 22, 2016).

Crawford, Sue E. S., and Elinor Ostrom. 1995. "A Grammar of Institutions." *American Political Science Review* 89(3): 582.

Demsetz, Harold. 1967. "Toward a Theory of Property Rights." *American Economic Review* 57(2): 347–59.

———. 1970. "The Private Production of Public Goods." *Journal of Law and Economics* 13(2): 293–306.

Dennett, Daniel C. 1989. *The Intentional Stance*, revised edn. Cambridge, MA: A Bradford Book.

———. 1991. "Real Patterns." *Journal of Philosophy* 88(1): 27–55.

———. 1995. *Darwin's Dangerous Idea: Evolution and the Meanings of Life*. New York: Simon & Schuster.

Devitt, Michael, and Kim Sterelny. 1999. *Language and Reality: An Introduction to the Philosophy of Language*, 2nd edn. Cambridge, MA: A Bradford Book.

Diamond, Jared M. 2005. *Collapse: How Societies Choose to Fail or Succeed*. New York: Penguin.

Dixit, Avinash. 2003. "Trade Expansion and Contract Enforcement." *Journal of Political Economy* 111(6): 1293–1317.

Easterly, William. 2002. *The Elusive Quest for Growth: Economists' Adventures and Misadventures in the Tropics*. Cambridge, MA: MIT Press.

————. 2007. *The White Man's Burden: Why the West's Efforts to Aid the Rest Have Done So Much Ill and So Little Good*, reprint edn. New York: Penguin Books.

————. 2015. *The Tyranny of Experts: Economists, Dictators, and the Forgotten Rights of the Poor*. Basic Books.

Elkin, Stephen L., and Karol Soltan, eds. 2007. *Citizen Competence and Democratic Institutions*. University Park, PA: Penn State University Press.

Fehr, Ernst, and Simon Gächter. 2002. "Altruistic Punishment in Humans." *Nature* 415(6868): 137–40.

Carl Folke, Steve Carpenter, Thomas Elmqvist, Lance Gunderson, C. S. Holling, and Brian Walker. 2002. "Resilience and Sustainable Development: Building Adaptive Capacity in a World of Transformations." *AMBIO: A Journal of the Human Environment* 31(5): 437–40.

Gao, Jianxi, Baruch Barzel, and Albert-László Barabási. 2016. "Universal Resilience Patterns in Complex Networks." *Nature* 530(7590): 307–12.

Gibson, Clark C., Krister Andersson, Elinor Ostrom, and Sujai Shivakumar. 2005. *The Samaritan's Dilemma: The Political Economy of Development Aid*. Oxford and New York: Oxford University Press.

Gibson, Clark C., Margaret A. McKean, and Elinor Ostrom, eds. 2000. *People and Forests: Communities, Institutions, and Governance*. Cambridge, MA: MIT Press.

Gintis, Herbert, Samuel Bowles, Robert Boyd, and Ernst Fehr. 2003. "Explaining Altruistic Behavior in Humans." *Evolution and Human Behavior* 24(3): 153–72.

Grube, Laura, and Virgil Henry Storr. 2013. "The Capacity for Self-Governance and Post-Disaster Resiliency." *Review of Austrian Economics* 27(3): 301–24.

Gunderson, Lance H. 2000. "Ecological Resilience—In Theory and Application." *Annual Review of Ecology and Systematics* 31: 425–39.

Hardin, Garrett. 1968. "The Tragedy of the Commons." *Science* 162(3859): 1243–48.

Hasnas, John. 2005. "Hayek, the Common Law, and Fluid Drive." *New York University Journal of Law and Liberty* 1: 79–110.

Hayek, Friedrich A. 1937. "Economics and Knowledge." *Economica* 4(13): 33–54.

————. 1945. "The Use of Knowledge in Society." *American Economic Review* 35(4): 519–30.

————. 1960. *The Constitution of Liberty*. Chicago, IL: University of Chicago Press.

————. 1973. *Law, Legislation and Liberty: Vol. 1. Rules and Order*. London and New York: Routledge.

————. 1989. "The Pretense of Knowledge." *American Economic Review* 79(6): 3–7.

Hess, Charlotte, and Elinor Ostrom. 2006. *Understanding Knowledge as a Commons: From Theory to Practice*. Cambridge, MA: MIT Press.

Hirschman, Albert O. 1970. *Exit, Voice, and Loyalty: Responses to Decline in Firms, Organizations, and States*. Cambridge, MA: Harvard University Press.

Holling, C. S. 1996. "Engineering Resilience versus Ecological Resilience." In *Engineering Within Ecological Constraints*, ed. Peter Schultze. Washington, DC: National Academies Press, 31–44.

Janssen, Marco A., John M. Anderies, and Elinor Ostrom. 2004. "A Framework to Analyze the Robustness of Social–Ecological Systems from an Institutional Perspective." *Ecology and Society* 9(1): 19.

———. 2007. "Robustness of Social–Ecological Systems to Spatial and Temporal Variability." *Society and Natural Resources* 20(4): 307–22.

Athena R. Kolbe, Royce A. Hutson, Harry Shannon, Eileen Trzcinski, Bart Miles, Naomi Levitz, Marie Puccio, Leah James, Jean Roger Noel & Robert Muggah. 2010. "Mortality, Crime and Access to Basic Needs before and after the Haiti Earthquake: A Random Survey of Port-Au-Prince Households." *Medicine, Conflict and Survival* 26(4): 281–97.

Kuran, Timur. 2005. "The Absence of the Corporation in Islamic Law: Origins and Persistence." *American Journal of Comparative Law* 53(4): 785–834.

La Porta, Rafael, Florencio Lopez-de-Silanes, and Andrei Shleifer. 2008. "The Economic Consequences of Legal Origins." *Journal of Economic Literature* 46(2): 285–332.

Labrousse, Agnès. 2016. "Not by Technique Alone. A Methodological Comparison of Development Analysis with Esther Duflo and Elinor Ostrom." *Journal of Institutional Economics* 12(2): 277–303.

Lansing, J. Stephen. 1991. *Priests and Programmers: Technologies of Power in the Engineered Landscape of Bali*. Princeton, NJ: Princeton University Press.

Lavoi, Don, and Emily Chamlee-Wright. 2001. *Culture and Enterprise: The Development, Representation and Morality of Business*. London and New York: Routledge.

Leeson, Peter T. 2014. *Anarchy Unbound: Why Self-Governance Works Better Than You Think*. Cambridge and New York: Cambridge University Press.

Leeson, Peter T., and Peter J. Boettke. 2009. "Two-Tiered Entrepreneurship and Economic Development." *International Review of Law and Economics* 29(3): 252–59.

Leonard, Mike. 2009. "The Story of Non-Economist Elinor Ostrom." *Herald-Times*.

Levine, Peter, and Karol Soltan, eds. 2014. *Civic Studies*. Washington, DC: Bringing Theory to Practice.

Lopez, German. 2016. "8 Shocking Findings from a City Task Force's Investigation into the Chicago Police Department." *Vox*. http://www.vox.com/2016/4/13/11424638/chicago-police-racism-report (May 11, 2016).

López, Edward, and Wayne Leighton. 2014. *Madmen, Intellectuals, and Academic Scribblers: The Economic Engine of Political Change.* Stanford, Calif.: Stanford Economics and Finance.

Lovett, Richard A. 2010. "Why Chile Fared Better than Haiti." *Nature: News Briefs.* http://www.nature.com/news/2010/100301/full/news.2010.100.html (February 5, 2016).

Mahoney, Paul G. 2001. "The Common Law and Economic Growth: Hayek Might Be Right." *Journal of Legal Studies* 30(2): 503–25.

Mäki, Uskali. 2005. "Models Are Experiments, Experiments Are Models." *Journal of Economic Methodology* 12(2): 303–15.

McGinnis, Michael D., ed. 1999a. *Polycentric Governance and Development: Readings from the Workshop in Political Theory and Policy Analysis.* Ann Arbor, MI: University of Michigan Press.

———, ed. 1999b. *Polycentricity and Local Public Economies: Readings from the Workshop in Political Theory and Policy Analysis.* Ann Arbor, MI: University of Michigan Press.

———. 2008. "Legal Pluralism, Polycentricity, and Faith-Based Organizations in Global Governance." In *The Struggle to Constitute and Sustain Productive Orders*, ed. Mark Sproule-Jones, Barbara Allen, and Filippo Sabetti. Lanham, MD: Lexington, 45–64.

———. 2010. "Religion Policy and the Faith-Based Initiative: Navigating the Shifting Boundaries between Church and State." *Forum on Public Policy* (4). http://forumonpublicpolicy.com/Vol2010.no4/religion2010.html.

———. 2011. "An Introduction to IAD and the Language of the Ostrom Workshop: A Simple Guide to a Complex Framework." *Policy Studies Journal* 39(1): 169–83.

———. 2016. "Polycentric Governance in Theory and Practice: Dimensions of Aspirations and Practical Limitations." Bloomington, IN: Indiana University.

McGinnis, Michael D., and James M. Walker. 2010. "Foundations of the Ostrom Workshop: Institutional Analysis, Polycentricity, and Self-Governance of the Commons." *Public Choice* 143(3/4): 293–301.

Miller, John H., and Scott E. Page. 2007. *Complex Adaptive Systems: An Introduction to Computational Models of Social Life.* Princeton, NJ: Princeton University Press.

Mitchell, William C. 1988. "Virginia, Rochester, and Bloomington: Twenty-Five Years of Public Choice and Political Science." *Public Choice* 56(2): 101–19.

Mokyr, J. 1990. *The Lever of Riches: Technological Creativity and Economic Progress.* New York: Oxford University Press.

Niskanen, Willam A. 1971. *Bureaucracy and Representative Government.* New Brunswick, NJ: Aldine Transaction.

North, Douglass C. 1990. *Institutions, Institutional Change and Economic Performance.* Cambridge and New York: Cambridge University Press.

Oakerson, Ronald J., and Roger B. Parks. 1988. "Citizen Voice and Public Entrepreneurship: The Organizational Dynamic of a Complex Metropolitan County." *Publius* 18(4): 91–112.

———. 2011. "The Study of Local Public Economies: Multi-Organizational, Multi-Level Institutional Analysis and Development: Oakerson/Parks: Study of Local Public Economies." *Policy Studies Journal* 39(1): 147–67.

Oates, Wallace E. 1972. *Fiscal Federalism*. Cheltenham, UK: Edward Elgar, 2007.

———. 1999. "An Essay on Fiscal Federalism." *Journal of Economic Literature* 37(3): 1120–49.

Olson, Mancur. 1965. *The Logic of Collective Action: Public Goods and the Theory of Groups*, revised edn, 1971. Cambridge, MA: Harvard University Press.

———. 1969. "The Principle of 'Fiscal Equivalence': The Division of Responsibilities among Different Levels of Government." *American Economic Review* 59(2): 479–87.

———. 1982. *The Rise and Decline of Nations: Economic Growth, Stagflation, and Social Rigidities*. New Haven, CT: Yale University Press.

———. 1996. "Big Bills Left on the Sidewalk: Why Some Nations Are Rich, and Others Poor." *Journal of Economic Perspectives* 10(2): 3–24.

Ostrom, Elinor. 1965. *Public Entrepreneurship: A Case Study in Ground Water Basin Management*. University of California–Los Angeles. PhD dissertation. https://dlc.dlib.indiana.edu/dlc/bitstream/handle/10535/3581/eostr001.pdf.

———. 1976a. "Multi-Mode Measures: From Potholes to Police." *Public Productivity Review* 1(3): 51–58.

———, ed. 1976b. *The Delivery of Urban Services: Outcomes of Change*. Beverly Hills, CA: Sage.

———. 1990. *Governing the Commons: The Evolution of Institutions for Collective Action*. Cambridge and New York: Cambridge University Press.

———. 1992. *Crafting Institutions for Self-Governing Irrigation Systems*. San Francisco, CA, and Lanham, MD: ICS Press.

———. 1996. "Crossing the Great Divide: Coproduction, Synergy, and Development." *World Development* 24(6): 1073–87.

———. 1998. "A Behavioral Approach to the Rational Choice Theory of Collective Action: Presidential Address, American Political Science Association, 1997." *American Political Science Review* 92(1): 1–22.

———. 1999a. "Polycentricity, Complexity, and the Commons." *Good Society* 9(2): 37–41.

———. 1999b. "Revisiting the Commons: Local Lessons, Global Challenges." *Science* 284(5412): 278–82.

———. 2000. "The Danger of Self-Evident Truths." *PS: Political Science and Politics* 33(Special Issue 1): 33–46.

————. 2005a. *Understanding Institutional Diversity*. Princeton, NJ: Princeton University Press.

————. 2005b. *Unlocking Public Entrepreneurship and Public Economies*. World Institute for Development Economics. Discussion Paper. http://www.econstor.eu/handle/10419/52899 (February 19, 2016).

————. 2007. "A Diagnostic Approach for Going beyond Panaceas." *Proceedings of the National Academy of Sciences* 104(39): 15181–87.

————. 2009. "A General Framework for Analyzing Sustainability of Social–Ecological Systems." *Science* 325: 419–22.

————. 2010a. "Beyond Markets and States: Polycentric Governance of Complex Economic Systems." *American Economic Review* 100(3): 641–72.

————. 2010b. "Polycentric Systems for Coping with Collective Action and Global Environmental Change." *Global Environmental Change* 20(4): 550–57.

————. 2011a. "Background on the Institutional Analysis and Development Framework." *Policy Studies Journal* 39(1): 7–27.

————. 2011b. "Honoring James Buchanan." *Journal of Economic Behavior and Organization* 80(2): 370–73.

————. 2012. *The Future of the Commons: Beyond Market Failure and Government Regulation*. London: Institute of Economic Affairs.

————. 2014. "Collective Action and the Evolution of Social Norms." *Journal of Natural Resources Policy Research* 6(4): 235–52.

Ostrom, Elinor, and Michael E. Cox. 2010. "Moving beyond Panaceas: A Multi-Tiered Diagnostic Approach for Social–Ecological Analysis." *Environmental Conservation* 37(4): 451–463.

Ostrom, Elinor, Roy Gardner, and Jimmy Walker. 1994. *Rules, Games, and Common-Pool Resources*. Ann Arbor, MI: University of Michigan Press.

Ostrom, Elinor, Marco A. Janssen, and John M. Anderies. 2007. "Going beyond Panaceas." *Proceedings of the National Academy of Sciences* 104(39): 15176–78.

Ostrom, Elinor, and Vincent Ostrom. 2004. "The Quest for Meaning in Public Choice." *American Journal of Economics and Sociology* 63(1): 105–47.

Ostrom, Elinor, Roger B. Parks, and Gordon P. Whitaker. 1974. "Defining and Measuring Structural Variations in Interorganizational Arrangements." *Publius* 4(4): 87–108.

————. 1978. *Patterns of Metropolitan Policing*. Ballinger Cambridge, MA.

Ostrom, Vincent. 1972. "Polycentricity (Part 1 and 2)." In *Polycentricity and Local Public Economies*, ed. Michael D. McGinnis. Ann Arbor MI: University of Michigan Press, 1999, 52-74-138.

————. 1973. *The Intellectual Crisis in American Public Administration*. Tuscaloosa, AL: University Alabama Press.

———. 1980. "Artisanship and Artifact." *Public Administration Review* 40(4): 309–17.

———. 1987. *The Political Theory of a Compound Republic: Designing the American Experiment*, 3rd revised edn. Lanham, MD: Lexington Books.

Vincent, Ostrom 1991b. 1991a. "Polycentricity: The Structural Basis of Self-Governing Systems." In *The Meaning of American Federalism*, San Francisco, CA: ICS Press, 223–48.

———. 1991b. *The Meaning of American Federalism*. San Francisco, CA: ICS Press.

———. 1993. "Epistemic Choice and Public Choice." *Public Choice* 77(1): 163–76.

———. 1997. *The Meaning of Democracy and the Vulnerabilities of Democracies: A Response to Tocqueville's Challenge*. Ann Arbor, MI: University of Michigan Press.

———. 2011. *The Quest to Understand Human Affairs, Vol. 1: Natural Resources Policy and Essays on Community and Collective Choice*, ed. Barbara Allen. Lanham, MD: Lexington Books.

———. 2012. *The Quest to Understand Human Affairs, Vol. 2: Essays on Collective, Constitutional, and Epistemic Choice*, ed. Barbara Allen. Lanham, MD: Lexington Books.

Ostrom, Vincent, Robert L. Bish, and Elinor Ostrom. 1988. *Local Government in the United States*. San Francisco, CA: ICS Press.

Ostrom, Vincent, and Elinor Ostrom. 1977. "Public Goods and Public Choices: The Emergence of Public Economies and Industry Structures." In *The Meaning of American Federalism*. San Francisco, CA: ICS Press, 1991, 163–97.

Ostrom, Vincent, Charles M. Tiebout, and Robert Warren. 1961. "The Organization of Government in Metropolitan Areas: A Theoretical Inquiry." *American Political Science Review* 55(4): 831–42.

Pahl-Wostl, Claudia, and Christian Knieper. 2014. "The Capacity of Water Governance to Deal with the Climate Change Adaptation Challenge: Using Fuzzy Set Qualitative Comparative Analysis to Distinguish between Polycentric, Fragmented and Centralized Regimes." *Global Environmental Change* 29: 139–54.

Roger B. Parks, Paula C. Baker, Larry Kiser, Ronald Oakerson, Elinor Ostrom, Vincent Ostrom, Stephen L. Percy, Martha B. Vandivort, Gordon P. Whitaker, Rick Wilson. 1981. "Consumers as Coproducers of Public Services: Some Economic and Institutional Considerations." *Policy Studies Journal* 9(7): 1001–11.

Peng, Xizhe. 1987. "Demographic Consequences of the Great Leap Forward in China's Provinces." *Population and Development Review* 13(4): 639–70.

Percy, Stephen L. 1984. "Citizen Participation in the Coproduction of Urban Services." *Urban Affairs Review* 19(4): 431–46.

Polanyi, Michael. 1951. *The Logic of Liberty*. London: Routledge.

———. 1962. "The Republic of Science: Its Political and Economic Theory." *Minerva* 1(1): 54–73.

Poteete, Amy R., Marco A. Janssen, and Elinor Ostrom. 2010. *Working Together: Collective Action, the Commons, and Multiple Methods in Practice*. Princeton, NJ: Princeton University Press.

Reisman, George. 1996. *Capitalism: A Treatise on Economics*. Ottawa, IL: Jameson Books.

Richard E. Wagner. 2014. "Entangled Political Economy: A Keynote Address." *Advances in Austrian Economics* 18: 15–36. http://www.emeraldinsight.com/doi/abs/10.1108/S1529-213420140000018000 (May 14, 2016).

Richerson, Peter J., and Robert Boyd. 2006. *Not by Genes Alone: How Culture Transformed Human Evolution*. Chicago, IL: University of Chicago Press.

Richey, Alexandra S., Brian F. Thomas, Min-Hui Lo, John T. Reager, et al. 2015. "Quantifying Renewable Groundwater Stress with GRACE." *Water Resources Research* 51(7): 5217–38.

Richey, Alexandra S., Brian F. Thomas, Min-Hui Lo, James S. Famiglietti, et al. 2015. "Uncertainty in Global Groundwater Storage Estimates in a Total Groundwater Stress Framework." *Water Resources Research* 51(7): 5198–216.

Ridley, Matt. 1996. *The Origins of Virtue: Human Instincts and the Evolution of Cooperation*. New York: Viking.

———. 2010. *The Rational Optimist: How Prosperity Evolves*. New York: Harper.

Rubin, Paul H. 1977. "Why Is the Common Law Efficient?" *Journal of Legal Studies* 6(1): 51–63.

Sabetti, Filippo. 2011. "Constitutional Artisanship and Institutional Diversity: Elinor Ostrom, Vincent Ostrom, and the Workshop." *Good Society* 20(1): 73–83.

Sabetti, Filippo, Barbara Allen, and Mark Sproule-Jones, eds. 2008a. *The Practice of Constitutional Development: Vincent Ostrom's Quest to Understand Human Affairs*. Lanham, MD: Lexington Books.

———, eds. 2008b. *The Struggle to Constitute and Sustain Productive Orders: Vincent Ostrom's Quest to Understand Human Affairs*. Lanham, MD: Lexington Books.

Samuelson, Paul A. 1954. "The Pure Theory of Public Expenditure." *Review of Economics and Statistics* 36(4): 387–89.

Schlager, Edella, and William Blomquist. 2008. *Embracing Watershed Politics*. Boulder, CO: University Press of Colorado.

Schlager, Edella, and Elinor Ostrom. 1992. "Property-Rights Regimes and Natural Resources: A Conceptual Analysis." *Land Economics* 68(3): 249–62.

Schmidtz, David. 2000. "The Institution of Property." In *The Common Law and the Environment: Rethinking the Statutory Basis for Modern Environmental Law*, ed. Roger E. Meiners and Andrew P. Morriss. Lanham, MD: Rowman & Littlefield, 109–29.

Searle, John R. 1969. *Speech Acts: An Essay in the Philosophy of Language*. London: Cambridge University Press.

———.1999 *Mind, Language and Society: Philosophy in the Real World*. New York: Basic Books.

Singleton, John D. 2015. "Sorting Charles Tiebout." *History of Political Economy* 47(suppl 1): 199–226.

Skyrms, Brian. 2003. *The Stag Hunt and the Evolution of Social Structure*. Cambridge, UK, and New York: Cambridge University Press.

Smith, Adam. 2009. "Elinor Ostrom Interview." *Nobel Media*. http://www.nobelprize.org/nobel_prizes/economic-sciences/laureates/2009/ostrom-telephone.html.

Sperber, Dan. 1996. *Explaining Culture: A Naturalistic Approach*, 1st edn. Oxford and Cambridge, MA: Blackwell.

Storr, Nona Martin, Emily Chamlee-Wright, and Virgil Henry Storr. 2015. *How We Came Back: Voices from Post-Katrina New Orleans*. Arlington, VA: Mercatus Center at George Mason University.

Storr, Virgil. 2015. Understanding the Culture of Markets. London and New York: Routledge.

Storr, Virgil Henry, and Nona Martin Storr. 2008. "On Perverse Emergent Orders." *Studies in Emergent Order* 1: 73–91.

Stringham, Edward Peter. 2015. *Private Governance: Creating Order in Economic and Social Life*. Oxford and New York: Oxford University Press.

Sullivan, Meg. 2011. "10 Questions for UCLA's Nobel Prize-Winning Economist Elinor Ostrom." *UCLA Newsroom*. http://newsroom.ucla.edu/stories/10-questions-for-nobel-prize-winning-200205 (Oct. 5th, 2016).

Tainter, Joseph. 1988. *The Collapse of Complex Societies*. Cambridge and New York: Cambridge University Press.

Tarko, Vlad. 2015a. "Polycentric Structure and Informal Norms: Competition and Coordination within the Scientific Community." *Innovation: European Journal of Social Science Research* 28(1): 63–80.

———. 2015b. "The Challenge of Empirically Assessing the Effects of Constitutions." *Journal of Economic Methodology* 22(1): 46–76.

———. 2015c. "The Role of Ideas in Political Economy." *Review of Austrian Economics* 28(1): 17–39.

Thierer, Adam. 2016. *Permissionless Innovation: The Continuing Case for Comprehensive Technological Freedom*, 2nd edn. Arlington, VA: Mercatus Center at George Mason University.

Tiebout, Charles M. 1956. "A Pure Theory of Local Expenditures." *Journal of Political Economy* 64(5): 416–24.

Tocqueville, Alexis de. 1835. *Democracy in America*. London: Penguin Classics.

Tomasello, Michael. 2009. *Why We Cooperate*. Cambridge, MA: MIT Press.

Toonen, Theo. 2010. "Resilience in Public Administration: The Work of Elinor and Vincent Ostrom from a Public Administration Perspective." *Public Administration Review* 70(2): 193–202.

Tullock, Gordon. 2005. *The Social Dilemma: Of Autocracy, Revolution, Coup d'Etat, and War*. Indianapolis, IN: Liberty Fund.

von Mises, Ludwig. 1949. *Human Action: A Treatise on Economics*. New Haven, CT: Yale University Press.

Wagner, Richard E. 2005. "Self-Governance, Polycentrism, and Federalism: Recurring Themes in Vincent Ostrom's Scholarly Oeuvre." *Journal of Economic Behavior and Organization* 57(2): 173–88.

Walker, Brian, C. S. Holling, Stephen Carpenter, and Ann Kinzig. 2004. "Resilience, Adaptability and Transformability in Social–Ecological Systems." *Ecology and Society* 9(2): 5.

Warren, Robert. 1966. *Government in Metropolitan Regions: A Reappraisal of Fractionated Political Organization*. Davis, CA: Institute of Government Affairs.

Warren, Robert. 1964. "A Municipal Services Market Model of Metropolitan Organization" *Journal of the American Institute of Planners* 30: 193–204.

Weingast, Barry R. 1995. "The Economic Role of Political Institutions: Market-Preserving Federalism and Economic Development." *Journal of Law, Economics, and Organization* 11(1): 1–31.

White, Lawrence H. 2012. *The Clash of Economic Ideas: The Great Policy Debates and Experiments of the Last Hundred Years*. New York: Cambridge University Press.

Williamson, Oliver E. 1975. *Markets and Hierarchies: Analysis and Antitrust Implications*. New York and London: Free Press.

———. 1992. "Markets, Hierarchies, and the Modern Corporation." *Journal of Economic Behavior and Organization* 17(3): 335–52.

———. 1996. *The Mechanisms of Governance*. Oxford: Oxford University Press.

———. 2009. "Pragmatic Methodology: A Sketch, with Applications to Transaction Cost Economics." *Journal of Economic Methodology* 16(2): 145–57.

Wilson, David Sloan. 2016. "The Woman Who Saved Economics from Disaster." *Evonomics*. http://evonomics.com/the-woman-who-saved-economics-from-disaster/ (May 9, 2016).

Wilson, David Sloan, Elinor Ostrom, and Michael E. Cox. 2013. "Generalizing the Core Design Principles for the Efficacy of Groups." *Journal of Economic Behavior and Organization* 90(Suppl): S21–32.

Zagorski, Nick. 2006. "Profile of Elinor Ostrom." *Proceedings of the National Academy of Sciences* 103(51): 19221–23.

Zhou, Tong, J. M. Carlson, and John Doyle. 2005. "Evolutionary Dynamics and Highly Optimized Tolerance." *Journal of Theoretical Biology* 236(4): 438–47.

# Index

189